Sewage Solutions
Answering the Call of Nature

by Nick Grant, Mark Moodie

and Chris Weedon

New Futures 12

CENTRE FOR
ALTERNATIVE
TECHNOLOGY
PUBLICATIONS

© September 1996
The Centre for Alternative Technology Machynlleth, Powys, SY20 9AZ, UK
Tel. 01654 702400 • **Fax**. 01654 702782
Email: cat@gn.apc.org • **Web page:** http://www.foe.co.uk/CAT

Assistance Peter Harper, Graham Preston,
Lesley Bradnam, Jules Lesniewski
Illustrations Graham Preston and Maritsa Kelly
Cover Photos *Main* Mark Moodie; *Background* Albatross Editions
Assistant Editor Julie Stauffer **Editor** Dave Thorpe

ISBN 1 898049 13 0
First Edition September 1996.

Mail Order copies from: Buy Green By Mail   Tel. 01654 703409
Trade Distribution: Biblios, Star Road, W. Sussex, RH13 8LD.   Tel. 01403 710 971

The details are provided in good faith and believed to be correct at the time of
writing, however no responsibility is taken for any errors. Our publications are updated
regularly; please let us know of any amendments or additions which you think may be
useful for future editions.
Printed on chlorine free paper obtained from sustainable sources.

Published with the invaluable assistance of Environment Wales,
a branch of the Welsh Office.

The Authors

Biographical notes on the authors by Peter Harper

Look, I know these guys. They are very singular characters. They come from different angles and do not always agree with each other. I have watched the whole thing from the sidelines and there's been a fair amount of blood on the carpet. Yet they passionately believe in the contents of this book *and apply it in their own lives* (sometimes to the distress of their partners, who are all long-suffering 'sewage widows'). They are intellectuals with a wide range of curiosities, yet they are also practical men, willing and able to get right up to their armpits in the stuff and make things work. They also share a dreadful taste for scatological wordplay, which I suppose must be an occupational hazard ...

Mark Moodie

Mark spent six years training in medicine and homoeopathy before getting into sewage in 1990. He operates the successful company, Camphill Water for the communities of Oaklands Park and The Grange. He comes to the subject from the distinctive anthroposophical angle with a strong emphasis on the homoeopathic qualities of water.

Nick Grant

Nick trained as a mechanical engineer, graduating from an unappetising 'thick sandwich with Paxman Diesels' to the more politically-focussed Engineering Design and Appropriate Technology at Warwick University. He met Mark while living in a community in Dorset, where they built their first reed bed system. They have been collaborating ever since.

Chris Weedon, B.Sc, A.R.C.S., D.I.C., Ph.D.

Chris is a biochemist who came to the Centre for Alternative Technology in 1992 from the pharmaceutical industry, where he had spent four years on research in microbial physiology. At the Centre he was in charge of the water supply and sewage treatment, while at home he developed a micro-reed bed system to treat his own family's sewage. Chris now works for Maltin Pollution Control Systems.

Contents

Foreword

A symptom of growing up, I think - potty talk matures (even degenerates) with age into excited discussions across urban and rural dinner tables of the pros and cons of human excrement. With wisdom comes a growing fascination with the multifarious ways of disposing of pooh....indeed, Christopher Robin probably has a lot to answer for in this matter, but that's grist for another treatise.

In my own work with the National Trust, I find that a good 75% of property management discussions revolve around the correct treatment of sewage.

And so they should — as a conservation issue the disposal of human waste is the most all-pervading cause of environmental health problems across the globe. As human populations expand, it is inevitable that the water each of us consumes or the land each of us uses will be affected by the effluent from all those people living 'upstream'. As our knowledge of the cyclic nature of the environment develops (with an increasing sense of urgency), we realise that the people who live 'downstream' of us also affect the health of our environment: through the sewage sludge that has to be disposed of; through the demand for water leading to more reservoirs and pipelines; and more insidiously through the acidification of lakes and streams from the deposition — in rainfall — of nitrogen derived from emissions from sewage disposal many miles away...

We have to be much cleverer in the way we regard human waste if we are going to solve some of the critical environmental problems of our time. We shall certainly have to invest in more water-efficient sewerage systems; we shall have to develop sewage treatment as a recycling process rather than a waste disposal process; we shall have to be much more selective about the kinds of waste which are put into sewage systems; above all, we have to change the all-too-common public attitude to waste - out of sight, out of mind (i.e. out of my site, out of my mind).

Thankfully, there is hope — a dedicated band of 'sewer-ers' is researching and applying new technologies to sewage treatment. This includes the three authors of this book and CAT and Camphill Water, for whom they work, but there are many others in commercial companies, water utilities, intermediate technology groups and universities who are persistently pushing new ideas and solutions into practice. The National Trust itself has taken a lead and installed dry compost lavatories, constructed wetland treatment systems, waterless urinals, 'Green cones' and improved septic tank systems at many of its properties. The benefits of these are apparent: a higher standard of water environment; reduced consumption of precious natural resources; and especially a greater awareness of the sensitivity of 'human effluent recycling systems' to damage from detergents, bactericides and inappropriate waste such as oils and grease and personal sanitary wear. These systems enable nutrients to be recycled as well as humus and water, so that a 'virtuous circle' of food production to healthy eating to return of natural resources to the environment can be established.

To all those who pick up this book to browse, YOU are the solution: "bon appetit" and "set to".

Rob Jarman
Environmental Practices Adviser
National Trust

Introduction

The Subject of this Book

During our daily work as designers of natural sewage treatment systems many people have approached us saying, "My septic tank is broken, I need a reed bed or pond system". Others have moved to the country and for the first time are faced with the unglamorous prospect of dealing with all the stuff they daily put down their drains, before it reaches the natural environment: "What do I do?"

Often a little information and orientation is all that is required to enable an old system to be brought back to its former glory. If you are in this position — seeking to upgrade an existing system — then we hope that *Sewage Solutions* will provide those insights.

The book is also intended as a first step for those who need a new system but who do not know what technological options are available, or what it would be useful to understand in order to make a sensible choice between the different possibilities.

Our main aim in writing this book has been to empower you to be able to choose and understand your own domestic sewage treatment system.

Our approach is first to provide a contextual framework for understanding the processes of sewage treatment within the those of life in general.

Assuming that you will be using a flush toilet (as opposed to other options), we move on to describe the basic principles of sewage treatment, followed by an account of the options for non-mains treatment, some of which are regarded as 'green' technologies and others — no less relevant — that are regarded as conventional.

This leads to a discussion of how to determine the extent to which your attempt at sewage treatment has been successful.

Then we go back a step to question the necessity of using water to transport human muck, and discuss the alternatives (such as compost toilets) and their associated benefits.

In a similar vein, we then deal with appropriate use of water in the home, which in itself can play a major role in determining your treatment system's design.

Finally we discuss the route by which treated sewage water can be re-introduced into the environment.

A Note on Vocabulary

The question of the appropriate terminology for bodily 'waste' has been widely debated both by the authors and elsewhere. There is nothing like sewage to invite toilet humour and witty puns, both of which we have chosen to avoid. But alternative names for faeces and urine are not free of dilemma. Should we be twee and tabloid, or blunt and widely understood. Perhaps we ought to stick to the terms of the scientific establishment and risk losing some folk to avoid offending others. But we would still have problems. For instance, the 'proper' term for a single coherent aggregate of faeces is not 'faece', but 'bolus' (a synonym for 'turd'); but does anyone out there actually use it?

There is no intention to offend with our choice of words. Nevertheless, there is an unavoidable down-to-earthness about sewage treatment systems. Not only must a spade be clearly labelled as such but, in the name of clarity so must all the other elements with which you will be dealing. We have tried to be varied and used plain old 'muck' as a general term, and the more technical 'faeces' or delicate 'poo' as alternatives to the Anglo-Saxon 'shit', whilst 'piss' and 'urine' are interchanged at random.

One term you may not be familiar with is 'humanure', intended to emphasise that properly treated human muck has potential for growing plants. When it comes down to it, shit by any other name will smell as sweet.

On a slightly different note, there is often confusion between 'sewage' and 'sewerage'. 'Sewage' is the stuff which is transported and treated by 'sewerage'. Sewerage is the term for the pipes, manholes, pumping stations and other hardware which enable all that sewage to get to its destination and be treated. Municipal scale sewerage is collectively known as 'the mains'.

Other specialised terms are discussed in the text and many are collected in the glossary.

A Warning About Pathogens

An organism is said to be pathogenic if it is implicated in a disease. If the disease is in a person, then we are dealing with a human pathogen. The faeces of healthy individuals contains vast numbers of bacteria, the majority of which are not pathogenic. However, a small proportion of the bacteria could cause stomach upset if ingested. Moreover, the excrement of people suffering certain diseases contains billions of pathogens. These include viruses (such as hepatitis A and polio virus), bacteria (such as those implicated in cholera and typhoid fever) and larger organisms (such as the protozoan associated with amoebic dysentery, or the flat-worm involved in river-blindness).

Due mainly to the improvements in municipal sanitation, serious water-borne diseases are extremely uncommon in the UK. However, ingestion of many species of bacteria commonly found in sewage-contaminated water can lead to stomach complaints, or worse if a kidney or other vital organ becomes infected.

The more intimate your contact with sewage the more chance you have of getting sick. Hygiene considerations strongly urge that you wear gloves and overalls if you have to work with sewage, and a face-mask to avoid splashing your mouth. After working with sewage avoid contact of clothing with the kitchen and eating areas and wash your hands thoroughly before eating. All basic common sense.

It is also important to take precautions to avoid transmission of disease by insects and other animals which might walk over our food after recently visiting sewage.

In much of the world (especially in hot climates), watercourses carry types of pathogens that can pass through intact skin. A very common example is the fluke or flatworm implicated in causing river blindness (Bilharzia, schistosomiasis).

Chapter One
The Big Circle

Before getting into the details and practicalities of choosing a sewage system it would be well to take a moment to get oriented. Having established the general context within which all sewage treatment occurs, one can focus more clearly upon some of the specific goals. Such a framework can be used to understand different sewage systems and evaluate their strengths and their shortcomings. The more one understands the rationale behind sewage treatment, the more creative one can be in devising sewage solutions.

The Big Circle

Sewage treatment is a specific case of a more general and ancient process. Inanimate matter (such as minerals, gases, water) is constantly being incorporated into organisms and so taken out of equilibrium with its environment. When they die, the organisms' bodies undergo a process of decay — returning closer to equilibrium with the inorganic world.

So for our purposes we can distinguish three phases of matter. In the first it is *mineral* or *inorganic*. When incorporated in the living tissues we can say matter is part of an *organism*. And when the organism dies we can say that it is *organic matter* until, once the process of decay has had its way, it is once again indistinguishable from the rest of the inorganic world.

This recycling of material, from dust and back to dust, is central to sustaining life and whether we are farmers, gardeners, or householders we are involved in this cycle — which we call the Big Circle (Fig.1.1). Sewage creators and treaters are no exception.

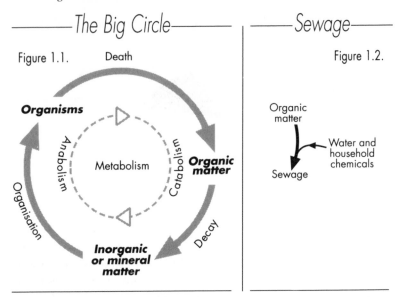

The Big Circle

Figure 1.1.

Sewage

Figure 1.2.

Sewage and the Big Circle

First of all, what is sewage? To be very general we can say domestic sewage is a mixture of water and the various types of organic matter which we send through the plumbing — faeces and urine, food scraps, hair, and toilet paper for example. Domestic sewage also contains household chemicals and detergents (Fig. 1.2), and we'll discuss these in detail in subsequent chapters.

For the majority of UK residents, all this stuff will disappear down various loos and plug holes, never to be seen by them again. These folks are 'on the mains', and the majority are required by law to connect to the municipal infrastructure. For historical reasons this makes a lot of sense, and we're not insisting that anyone break free from the mains.

But for those not on the mains and who want (or are compelled) to do 'the right thing' with their wastewater, what happens after the flush needs to be considered too. That's what this book is all about.

Sewage Breakdown and the Mineral Solution

Once the sewage disappears down those loos and plug holes, as with all organic matter, it breaks down. The complex organisation that was, for example, a cabbage undergoes a series of processes

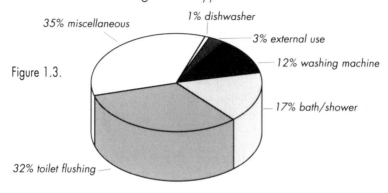

—————— Water Usage in a Typical Household ——————

35% miscellaneous

1% dishwasher

3% external use

Figure 1.3.

12% washing machine

17% bath/shower

32% toilet flushing

which make it less and less recognisable as cabbage and more and more akin to the breakdown products of other organic bits of sewage — for instance, former carrots or faeces.

At all stages of breakdown of our cabbage some 'energy' is released. We get energy when we eat the cabbage. When we excrete it our so-called 'wastes' become a feast — a source of energy — for other tiny creatures. These microorganisms will go to work, breaking the organic matter down into smaller and simpler fragments, and producing heat.

The breakdown occurs only as far and as fast as conditions allow. If these are right, the creatures will continue to break down our wastes, releasing various gaseous products. Eventually all that is left is a solution of minerals dissolved in water. These minerals are stable — unless prevailing conditions change they will not break down any further.

The process of breaking down organic waste is often called 'mineralisation' (Fig. 1.4). The process is also known as digestion, catabolism, disintegration, or dissolution and is desirable in a sewage treatment system (and in the next chapter we'll say why this is so).

Conditions for digestion

What are the conditions required to turn the sewage into a mineral solution as efficiently and completely as possible? The answer is the presence of sufficient heat and oxygen. Given the

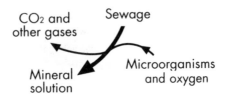

Figure 1.4.

right proportions of the four ingredients — organic matter ('earth'), heat ('fire'), oxygen ('air'), and water — a wide array of tiny creatures will make sure that the sewage decays. And that's the bare bones of sewage treatment.

To help understand why each ingredient is crucial, consider what we could do to preserve sewage. If we were to remove heat by freezing it we would get a rather stable if unsavoury ice cube. If we were to remove the water by desiccating it, we would be left with a pot-noodle which might even threaten the market. Should we remove the air, by pickling or fermenting it, we would have something like sauerkraut. Finally, should we remove the organic matter, we would be left with clean water.

It is also instructive to consider what would happen if we played around with the proportions of the four ingredients. We will consider this in chapter five, for this is precisely where lie the practice and science of sewage treatment.

There's one very common misapprehension worth correcting here — that sewage treatment simply means removing material from water. It does not; it is its *transformation* which is important. Apart from the greater part of the carbon (which leaves as carbon dioxide), the mineral solution at the end will contain a great deal of the same atoms of stuff as the sewage did before the bugs started breaking it down. (It is possible to remove minerals from the solution, but this is a complex proposition that is picked up in chapters two and seven.)

Reintegration

The story does not end here though. *Catabolism* is only part of the cycle of metabolism — the Big Circle. The other half is *anabolism*

─────── Box 1.2. What-o-trophs? ───────

Bacteria need both an energy source and a carbon source for cell material. To produce their energy they can use light (in which case they are called 'phototrophs') or chemical compounds ('chemotrophs'). To build their cell material the carbon can come from either organic material ('heterotrophs') or CO_2 ('autotrophs'). Combinations of all four groups exist, giving a rich variety of metabolic types.

Category	Energy source	carbon source	Examples
Photoautotroph	light	CO_2	photosynthetic bacteria (all green plants)
Photoheterotroph	light	organic C	some purple and green bacteria
Chemoautotroph	chemicals	CO_2	nitrifying bacteria
Chemoheterotroph	chemicals	organic C	most bacteria, fungi, animals

— the construction of organisms from simple minerals (see Fig.1.1). Let's go back to the mineral state. We stated that the minerals are stable, and this is true — they will not break down into smaller fragments. But their environment is full of potential, one in which creatures can live the good life, multiply and grow.

Best adapted to using the raw components of the mineral solution are plants and microorganisms. They find it very nutritious and for this reason the output of a sewage treatment system is sometimes called a nutrient solution. Microorganisms have many methods of getting what they need for energy and growth. These have been used to categorise bacteria into different groups (Box 1.2).

Given some encouragement — like warmth, light, and air — they will help the solution change colour, and become organised. The first organisms to join the feast will be relatively simple

The Ascending Limb

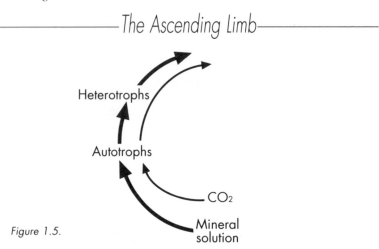

Figure 1.5.

autotrophs. These will become food for the first heterotrophic organisms which in turn become food for further heterotrophs. Holding such a solution before the mind's eye, one would see phyto-plankton and zoo-plankton. Then would appear more complex organisms: micro-invertebrates, larger plants, insects and their larvae, amphibia and fish. Without imaginative restraint, from out of the liquid leaps a whale. Not only do whales appear, but also organisms that can live around the aquatic solution: terrestrial mammals and birds, and even organisations who are so complex they have complexes — us.

We can call this ascending limb, creation, organisation, integration, or anabolism (Fig. 1.5).

Experience shows that this orgy of growth, eating and being eaten, multiplication and specialisation cannot continue unabated. Everyone who joins the party leaves it at some time. At death, the integrity of the organisation begins to break down, form fades away, ability to reproduce is lost, and the ability of the corpse of a cabbage, parrot, or human to demonstrate consciousness (let alone responsible decision making) is zero. Not all of these carcasses will find their way into sewage but everything that does will have been part of this cycle (Fig. 1.6).

The Big Sewage Circle

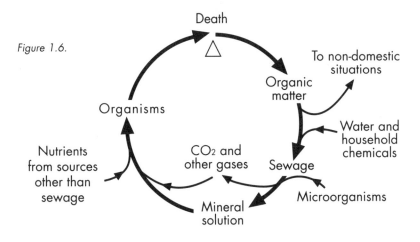

Figure 1.6.

Using the Big Circle

The map is not the same as the territory. For example, the downward half of the cycle is not always completed by each carcass before it is swept up into a new organism. Were we to allow for this and all other variations on the theme we would have to employ animation, and something like a writhing bowl of spaghetti would appear, rather than an orderly static circle. The Big Sewage Circle is not immutable law but an aid to understanding what happens as organic matter breaks down in water.

We have assumed that the reader wishes to use this as a guide to responsible interaction with this cycle. The Circle enables us to see what we might manipulate and change, what it would be foolish to change, and what it would be foolish to leave alone.

For instance, we might ask ourselves at what point in the cycle we should release our treated sewage back to the wider world in a particular situation, or whether we could reintroduce the mineral solution back into the cycle at some other point. Would we add the mineral solution to food crops as a fertilising irrigant or are there problems with this?

We can ask ourselves why we added the water to the organic matter to begin with and, assuming we decided that this was an appropriate thing to do, what would be a sensible amount and quality of water. One can place various schools of sewage treatment and various pieces of sewage-treating equipment on to the map and see how they fit into the whole. Questions of finance, understanding, level of interest and taboo can be inserted in various points and the map changes about its basic form. Feel free to play.

Summary

All matter on Earth is in a process of continuous transformation — the 'Big Circle'.

Inanimate matter can be incorporated into life — vitalised — after which it returns to the inanimate state by processes of disintegration. Disintegration may occur either at the death of the organism or after expulsion of matter from the organism. Since, in the case of humans, expulsion of waste bodily matter is often to water, this complicates the picture. Hence we have presented you with the 'Big Sewage Circle', a model in which general principles of sewage treatment and its relationship to the wider environment can be illustrated.

Chapter Two
Treating Sewage

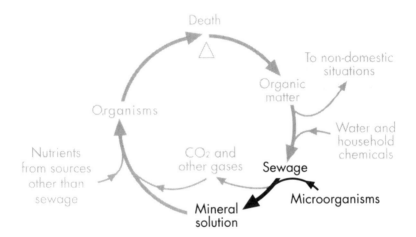

The Big Circle set the scene for our discussion of sewage. We have seen that the contaminants in our wastewater are transformed, becoming incorporated into living organisms, and that if humans are involved, sewage can eventually be re-generated. So the same material cycles round and round continuously, occasionally being added to water by humans, producing sewage.

This chapter deals with the processes by which sewage is transformed, thus cleaning the water — sewage treatment. These processes involve first transforming the constituents of the sewage into inorganic form, followed by removing these mineral constituents, reintroducing them back into living organisms. Some of the main impurities can be removed by certain bacteria, which convert the dissolved material into harmless gaseous products. Such a process is commonly attempted in conventional sewage treatment. Other constituents are readily taken up as nutrients into

———Box 2.1. What is in domestic sewage———

Everything that people put down their toilets and drains from sinks, washing machines, etc, becomes sewage. Unfortunately, some people mistakenly treat their drains as another dustbin! Sewage bits include:

Screenable solids (big lumps of material that can be removed from the water by a coarse screen): paper (lavatory paper, paper towels, etc.), food particles, tampons, sanitary towels, condoms, nappy liners, incontinency pads and bags, a myriad other non-biodegradable sanitary items (ear-buds, plastic wrappers, etc.)

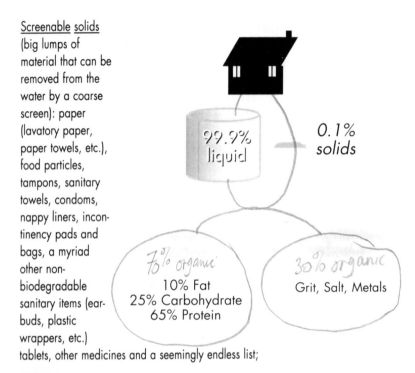

99.9% liquid

0.1% solids

7% organic
10% Fat
25% Carbohydrate
65% Protein

30% organic
Grit, Salt, Metals

tablets, other medicines and a seemingly endless list;

Non-screenable solids (tiny particles, most of which remain suspended indefinitely in water and which give it a cloudy appearance): bacteria, faecal particles, food particles, fats, oils and greases, detergents and soaps, washings (from clothes, skin from bodies, etc.), sediment;

Dissolved material (which may contribute colour but not cloudiness): organic matter: proteins, urea (from urine), carbohydrates, fatty acids, other organic molecules in small amounts (DNA, etc.), and ions of ammonia, chloride, nitrate and nitrite, phosphate, sulphide, minerals, metals and trace elements, other inorganic molecules in small amounts (vitamins, etc.).

plants. It is common practice to leave this job to the organisms of the natural environment, but it can be achieved in a controlled manner with great benefit. We will return to this topic in chapter seven.

Why Treat Sewage?

We stated in the previous chapter that microorganisms break down the organic matter in sewage, and that these microorganisms require oxygen for their respiration. These little creatures are extremely efficient at getting oxygen if there is any available. In fact, they are much more efficient than the more highly evolved creatures that live in unpolluted streams, such as fish.

This brings us to the first reason for treating sewage. If you ran a pipe from your house to the nearest stream and dumped your domestic sewage directly into it, the microorganisms would use up all the oxygen dissolved in the stream water as they broke down that sewage.

The organic matter would get broken down but there would be no oxygen for fish. To protect the fish, and various other aquatic organisms that depend on having oxygen in the water, the organic matter in your sewage must be digested before it reaches your local stream.

Because organic matter uses oxygen when decomposing, the amount of organic matter in a body of water can be conveniently ascertained by measuring how much oxygen is being removed (i.e. demanded by the microorganisms present) from the water. This measurement is known as the Biochemical Oxygen Demand (BOD).

Another readily testable measurement for the amount of matter – called 'suspended solids' (SS) – in sewage is to see how much is caught in a filter. If discharged to a stream the solids would obscure light, even if none of them were susceptible to digestion.

SS and BOD are the two qualities of sewage most commonly measured by the authorities.

Another reason for sewage treatment is that sewage contains potentially pathogenic materials and organisms; bacteria, viruses, worms and chemical compounds. The need for effective sewage treatment is clear when one considers that near the mouth of some

———*Box 2.2. Metabolism in sewage treatment*———

End products of aerobic and anaerobic decomposition (simplified)

Element	Aerobic	Anaerobic
carbon C	carbon dioxide CO_2	methane CH_4
hydrogen H	water H_2O	hydrogen H_2
oxygen O	oxygen O_2	water H_2O
nitrogen N	nitrate NO_3^-	ammonia NH_3
phosphorus P	phosphate PO_4^{3-}	phosphane PH_3
sulphur S	sulphate SO_4^{2-}	hydrogen sulphide H_2S

rivers, people are drinking water that has previously quenched the thirst of many others.

Aerobic or Anaerobic?

To reiterate the aims: the first step is to transform the organic matter into the mineral constituents; the next step is to remove them from the water. To achieve these goals we must create conditions in which the organic matter can be digested by microorganisms: sufficient moisture, warmth and air. Moisture is not short in a water-borne sewage system. Warmth is sometimes lacking — especially in winter — but in the UK climate the temperature within a system rarely becomes low enough to completely halt degradation.

Oxygen, unlike the other factors, can easily be in short supply and careful provision must be made to ensure sewage has good access to it. Degradation can occur in the absence of oxygen (anaerobic conditions) but the metabolic processes involved are much slower than in the presence of oxygen (aerobic conditions). The range of metabolic processes is complicated but we can generalise by saying that in aerobic conditions the chemical elements will emerge from the degradation process in combination with oxygen; in anaerobic conditions they will emerge combined with hydrogen (Box 2.2).

The products of aerobic decomposition are odourless, non-toxic and water soluble. They represent full breakdown of the various contaminants of sewage water and are therefore stable. They are the constituents of the mineral solution.

Some products of anaerobic degradation, such as alcohols and fatty acids are more chemically complicated than those shown in Box 2.1. Many are toxic to organisms adapted to conditions in an oxygen-rich environment. Some are noxious gases like hydrogen sulphide and methane. Some of the gases are potentially explosive. A notable feature of most anaerobic products is that they are smelly. One always knows when there is insufficient oxygen available for the aerobic breakdown of sewage through one's nose.

Furthermore, methane in particular is far more potent as a greenhouse gas than its aerobic counterpart, carbon dioxide. To help limit global warming and resultant climate chaos it should therefore be avoided.

The whole anaerobic gas mixture is sometimes referred to as 'biogas'. Anaerobic digestion at quite high temperatures (typically around 35°C). Nevertheless, anaerobic digesters are commonly used to break down sewage in warmer climates although in the UK they are economically viable only on a large scale. Anaerobic breakdown of organic matter is common in nature, occurring in bogs for instance.

Treatment Stages

Sewage treatment systems are characterised by the level of treatment they provide:

Preliminary Treatment

Preliminary treatment involves the physical removal of relatively large or heavy solids (grit, wood, rags, old bicycles, etc). This is usually achieved by passing the incoming sewage through a screen with bars 25-50 mm apart (see Fig 2.1), or through a net of similar gauge. The methods are exclusively physical, and very little organic contamination has been diverted from the liquid. So the BOD is not much reduced.

Preliminary treatment is rarely required for the domestic sized systems, unless there are pumps which lift the raw and unsettled sewage.

Preliminary Screening

Figure 2.1. Preliminary screening at the small treatment plant of an army barracks.

Primary Treatment

Primary treatment usually involves slowing the sewage down by putting the effluent into a chamber so the suspended solids (mainly organic material) settle to the bottom of the chamber through the force of gravity, or float to the surface by buoyancy. This process is also predominantly physical. Since the material that settles out is organic, the total BOD of the sewage which continues through the system is reduced.

In domestic situations, this settlement chamber is usually a septic tank, where gross solids settle or float thus removing around 30–50% of the BOD and SS. The effluent from this stage is still highly polluting and if you were to collect some in a jam-jar you would notice that it is a fairly opaque grey colour with a distinctly sewagey smell (Fig 2.2, left hand jam-jar).

Secondary Treatment

This process removes most of the remaining BOD (mainly soluble organic material) and SS. It is also known as biological treatment since it depends on microorganisms breaking down the

Jam-jar Sampling

Figure 2.2. Jam-jars of sewage after (left) passage through a septic tank and after (right) good secondary treatment (settled).

organic material in the sewage. Given the right conditions, microorganisms will thrive in the effluent of primary treatment and, in feeding on it, break it down. In simple terms, biological sewage treatment — or secondary treatment — is all about creating an environment where this can happen at an accelerated rate, in a relatively small space, away from valuable habitats such as trout streams. A sample of effluent from a secondary stage will, if all is well, show that our smelly grey soup has been transformed into a fairly clear liquid.

If we allow the slightly turbid secondary effluent to stand for a few hours, any remaining solids settle out, leaving the final product of secondary treatment; a clear 'mineral solution'.

We can achieve settling of the secondary solids by adding a second settling tank and the result is an effluent that should satisfy the regulatory authorities (Fig. 2.2, right hand jam-jar).

Whilst the details vary we can summarise the recipe for secondary biological treatment system as:

1. Somewhere for the bugs to live

2. A source of oxygen
3. A way of removing the dead microorganisms (settlement tank).

Tertiary Treatment

Tertiary treatment refers to any or all of the following:
• Removal of further remaining BOD and SS;
• Removal of nutrients, i.e. nitrogen and phosphorus compounds;
• Removal of pathogenic organisms.

This can all involve physical, biological, and/or chemical processes. The chemical treatment may be flocculation of the phosphorus, which is followed by the physical act of settlement and separation. Some people use this term to refer specifically to only one of the above changes to the sewage. Generally, though, tertiary treatment is used quite vaguely to refer to any combination of the above.

Tertiary treatment is only sometimes attempted or insisted upon by the regulatory authorities. It is usual for a sewage treatment plant to discharge secondary quality water, leaving further clean-up of this water to the organisms in the natural environment. Nevertheless, legal standards are rising all the time and there are obvious ecological benefits in ensuring that as much treatment as possible is achieved before wastewater reaches the natural environment.

Tertiary treatment usually involves taking the mineral solution through a further biological, physical or chemical step. On a municipal scale, dissolved contaminants can be economically removed by precipitation (the solids being chemically forced out of solution), flocculation and settlement.

A range of existing technologies and possible formats will be covered in some detail in chapter three.

Summary

Domestic sewage is a mixture created by a human activity of disposing unwanted household materials to water.

In order to minimise the adverse affects of sewage on the environment and on people, it is necessary to treat the dissolved and suspended constituents in the water. This involves first removing gross particles (primary treatment), then — mainly biologically — transforming the constituents into stable, 'mineral' form (secondary treatment). Further removal by physical, chemical and/or biological means is possible (tertiary treatment).

Chapter Three
Sewage Treatment Systems

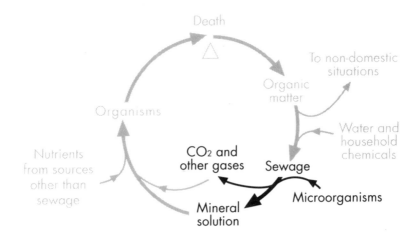

Having looked at the context for sewage treatment and introduced you to the basic processes involved, we now turn our attention to the hardware involved in small scale, on-site treatment of sewage. The chapter is arranged as follows:

1. Choosing a treatment system
2. Small scale sewage treatment technologies
3. If it ain't broke, don't fix it.

Choosing a Treatment System

To guide the transformation of raw sewage to mineral solution in the Big Circle, and to do this in a way that is efficient and acceptable to society, means making use of several processes and bits of equipment which satisfy the basic requirements we have sketched out in the preceding chapters.

Any good sewage treatment system must take into account a number of principal factors. The least you must do is to ensure that the system will meet the standards set by the relevant local authorities. After that come various factors, the importance of which varies with each individual situation:

- space availability
- level of maintenance you are prepared and able to give
- degree of smell and aesthetic impact you will tolerate
- ecological sensitivity of the site
- amount of money you can spend on it
- power requirements and availability
- whether you wish to build the system yourself or want to buy one 'off the shelf'
- who might use the property next.

A starting place and reference point for choosing the most suitable treatment system is the Designer's Checklist of System Types and the Designer's Flowchart beginning on page 114. The Flowchart gives a broad summary of one possible decision making process and the Checklist gives the different characteristics of the various systems and many of the factors we think you may want to consider.

In this chapter we briefly describe each method or technology with the aim of allowing you to compare them and decide which one is for you. Note that each different method is rarely more than part of a whole sewage treatment system. Where individual elements are commonly used together (e.g. septic tank and leachfield), this is stated. However, almost any combination is possible (although we hope it will be clear that it would be foolish, for instance, to have a bark ring receiving the effluent of a solar pond).

Sewage Treatment Technologies

These are the technologies to be discussed:

1. Cesspools
2. Septic tanks
3. Settlement tanks
4. Bark rings
5. Percolating filters
6. Package plants
7. Vertical flow reed beds

8. Horizontal flow reed beds
9. Solar ponds
10. Leachfields
11. Willows and trenches
12. Living machines

1. Cesspools

A cesspool (Fig. 3.1) is a very big tank (at least 18 m³), that has an inlet but no outlet, and in this way differs from a septic tank. Cesspools do not treat sewage, but simply store it until it is removed by a sludge tanker. Where the ground is unsuitable for accepting discharged water and in places where no receiving watercourse is available, they are the only conventional solution.

A typical four-person family will produce around 700 litres of sewage a day and an average tanker can hold 8,000–12,000 litres. This means that a tanker load must be removed every two weeks at a cost of around £100–200 a time (1996 prices; depends on distance tankered, locality, etc). So radical water conservation, dry toilets and greywater irrigation will show a very quick payback.

Cesspools are often installed because of high groundwater tables and thus any leaks in the tank can mean it will fill with clean water leaving no room for the sewage.

Pros:
- May be the only conventional solution in some areas
- On-site pollution is zero
- DIY is possible (see *Septic Tanks and Cesspools*, P. Jobling; in the Resource Guide)
- Nothing to go wrong other than leaks or overflow.

Cons:
- Transport and final disposal have high ecological impact
- Emptying is expensive and costs continue to increase
- May not be permitted for new developments in some areas.

2. Septic tanks

These are often confused with cesspools but cesspools have an inlet but no outlet, while septic tanks have both. Septic tanks (Fig. 3.2) are much smaller than cesspools because they retain only the equivalent of around a day's worth of flow. Septic tanks must be

Cesspool

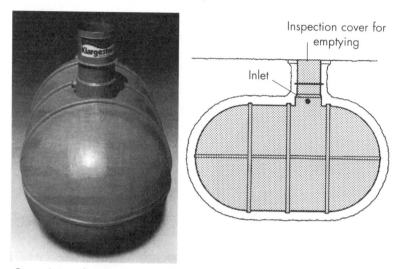

Inspection cover for
emptying

Inlet

Figure 3.1.a. Photograph of a prefabricated cesspool (not installed) (courtesy of Klargester Environmental Engineering Ltd.).
Figure 3.1.b. Side view of a Prefabricated Cesspool (courtesy of Klargester Environmental Engineering Ltd.).

sized according to the number of people served, but the regulations (BS.6297 and Building Regulations) recommend that a septic tank should be no smaller than 2,700 litres.

A septic tank often has one or two chambers. Raw sewage enters the first chamber, where most of the solids either settle or float leaving the clearer liquid between, to pass out of the tank or on to the next chamber for further settlement. The incoming wastewater simply displaces the water already in the tank in the same way that a bath would overflow were one to leave the tap running. Do not be surprised therefore, when looking inside, to find it 'full '. When water is displaced from the final chamber, most of the gross solids and about one third to one half of the organic load have been retained as sludge and floating crust, which must be removed periodically (from every six months to every six years) by sludge tanker. The optional job of removing and composting the

Septic tank

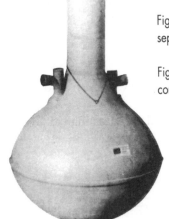

Figure 3.2.a. Photograph of a prefabricated septic tank (not installed).

Figure 3.2.b. (below) Cross-section of a constructed septic tank.

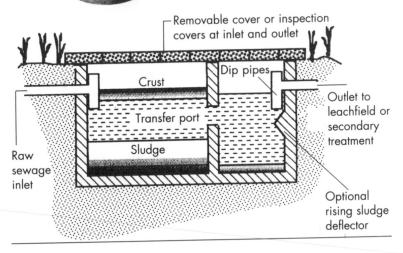

floating material, known invitingly as the crust, is fully described in the sister publication *Fertile Waste* (see Resource Guide).

Septic tanks only provide primary treatment and so should be followed by a leachfield or secondary treatment system.

There is little to go wrong, other than blockages which are common to any primary stage, but check that the dip pipe has not fallen off as this will allow solids to be discharged, which will overload the leachfield or treatment system. Very often leachfield failure is blamed on the septic tank although it is usually the leachfield that has become blocked or overloaded. All aspects are discussed in *Septic Tanks: an Overview* (see Resource Guide).

Pros:
- Little to go wrong
- Established technology
- Low head loss
- DIY is possible (see *Septic Tanks and Cesspools*, P. Jobling)
- Underground, so almost invisible
- Prefabricated tanks can be installed in less than a day
- Low cost compared with other primary treatment.

Cons:
- Often misunderstood
- Only primary treatment; must not discharge to watercourse
- Must be desludged regularly (despite stories to the contrary)
- Effluent is anaerobic, so will usually smell.

3. Settlement tanks

Similar to septic tanks but a lot smaller — holding up to 8 hours equivalent flow (Fig. 3.3), settlement tanks' main advantage for raw sewage is that the effluent is less likely to be fully anaerobic and smelly. For them to work effectively the sludge must be removed at least every two weeks so you need to treat sludge on site. Also, because Building Control will want the tank to be at the very least 2,700 litres, settlement is not really suitable for populations of less than 30 or so. Specialist advice should be sought before installing primary settlement tanks.

Smaller settlement tanks are used further down the system for removing 'humus solids' from the water stream. These are called secondary solids tanks or humus settlement tanks (see trickling filters below).

Pros:
- Provides primary treatment (or secondary solids removal)
- Effluent should not be septic or smell 'too bad'
- Smaller and cheaper than septic tanks for big systems
- Humus tanks can be desludged by pump to primary stage
- Low head loss

Cons:
- Require frequent sludge removal.

Settlement tank

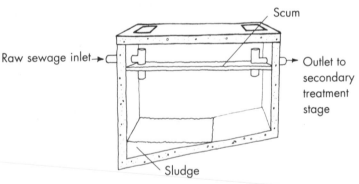

Figure 3.3.a. A constructed settlement tank (Eco-cabins system, CAT).
Figure 3.3.b. Cross-section of a settlement tank.

4. Bark rings

These are large chambers often built using concrete rings partially filled with rough, porous, carbonaceous material such as straw or tree bark (hence the name). Raw sewage enters at the top of the tank and falls on to the carbonaceous material (Fig. 3.4). The system achieves primary treatment by physical filtration whilst the

Bark ring

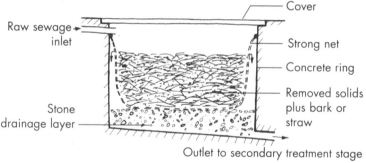

Figure 3.4.a. Photograph of a bark ring (site system, CAT).
Figure 3.4.b. Cross-section of a bark ring.

water receives some secondary treatment within the structure of the bark. The tank is designed to collect a few months', or as much as two years', worth of solids. Attached to the walls of the tank is a cargo net, which is fine enough to retain the original bark and strong enough to carry the whole pile when it is time to empty the tank. Underneath the net is a layer of stones, which ensures good drainage. The tanks are usually installed in pairs to allow one to rest and mature whilst the second is 'on line'. In this way, close personal contact with fresh material is avoided, even during removal.

This method is a recent innovation, still being optimised by a handful of users, including CAT, Camphill Water, and The Highgrove Estate of Prince Charles. The same basic process is used by the DOWMUS, which is described on page 107 in chapter five.

Pros:
- Provides primary treatment
- Aerobic effluent
- In-situ composting of solids possible with correct design
- Removal and retrieval of organic solids early in process
- Solids can be removed by shovel, so ideal where no tanker access.

Cons:
- Requires close contact with raw sewage when emptying
- Need regular additions of soak, e.g. straw, cardboard, bark
- Little-known technology in UK
- Requires a fall of around 1.5–2 metres (or pump for effluent)
- Correct sizing crucial to avoid blockage
- More expensive than septic tank
- Requires management and user awareness
- At present, suitable only for enthusiasts and special situations.

5. Percolating filters

Also known as trickling filters, biological filters, biofilters, clinker beds, rotating arm systems, bacteria beds and filter beds. Percolating filters (Fig. 3.5) are always preceded by a primary settlement stage, usually a septic tank and followed by a humus tank.

A percolating filter is a container, typically 1.2 to 2.0 m deep, usually filled with blast furnace clinker or stones. This material is generically known as the matrix. Sewage is distributed over the surface of this matrix, and drains freely from the base. Distribution is typically achieved by a rotating arm driven by the in-coming water, although smaller systems often use a rectangular tank and a tipping trough, as shown in Fig. 3.5. The sewage clings as a thin

Percolating filter

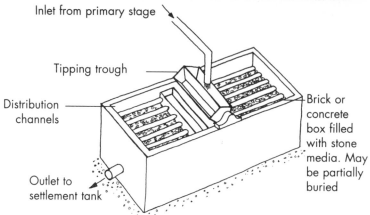

Inlet from primary stage

Tipping trough

Distribution channels

Brick or concrete box filled with stone media. May be partially buried

Outlet to settlement tank

Figure 3.5.a. Photograph of a percolating filter and primary settlement tank for a small rural community.
Figure 3.5.b. Schematic of a small domestic percolating filter with tipping trough.

film to the surface of the matrix, a phenomenon known as the Coanda effect. In this thin nutritious layer, surrounded by plenty of air, microorganisms thrive and multiply, forming a slime known as the biofilm or zooglial film (after one of the commonest bacteria in the film, *Zoogloea*). It is the contact with the microbes in the biofilm that cleans the water — the bugs literally digest the organic matter in the water. As this biofilm gets thicker the inner layers of bugs attached to the stones are smothered and die and the biofilm is loosened from its anchor. This process of 'sloughing off' is aided by a range of larger organisms that graze on the film. The sloughed material can be removed from the liquid in a secondary settlement tank, leaving a clear liquid fit for discharge (as described in chapter two).

As with other biological treatment systems, the microorganisms can be killed if poisonous substances are put into the sewage system. In this, respect trickling filters are generally considered more robust than activated sludge or package plants but less biologically robust than vertical flow reed beds.

Pros:
- Relatively robust
- Tried and tested
- Does not require power if a fall is available.

Cons:
- If the mechanism jams, treatment effectively stops
- Expensive
- Rarely used today for single household systems
- Tipper type can be noisy
- Requires regular maintenance
- Needs a fall of 1.5–2m or a pump
- Regular de-sludging of humus tank and septic tank crucial to ensure good effluent
- Usually placed some distance from dwellings
- Biofilm will die off if system is unused for long periods
- Can block if overloaded.

6. Package Plants

Package plants (Fig. 3.6) are 'off-the-shelf' treatment systems for treating raw or primary treated sewage. Package plants can be installed quickly, often in a day, and are relatively compact. They are widely used and well established, with maintenance support usually available from the supplier.

The main variations are outlined below but all involve settling the solids before and/or after an aerobic biological stage, and all use an electrical power input.

Features common to all package plants:
Pros:
• Compact
• Fast installation
• Do not require a gradient fall
• Medium cost (comparatively) for secondary treatment
• As close to 'fit and forget' as is presently available
• Maintenance contract available from installer
• Can be made invisible as mostly buried in ground
• Return of humus solids to the primary stage is a good feature.
Cons:
• Need electricity supply
• Use electricity (amount varies between models)
• Require regular maintenance for proper function
• Not DIY
• Slight noise of some designs may cause annoyance
• Not generally tolerant of short term overload
• Small size limits buffering effect
• No treatment in the event of a power cut or following mechanical failure
• Large amount of secondary solids created.
Other Comments:
• Once to twice yearly sludge removal required
• A horizontal flow reed bed will often improve effluent quality
• May incorporate primary settlement in same package.

6.1 Rotary biological contactors

Also called RBCs or biodiscs (Fig. 3.6.1), these hold a series of high surface area discs, mounted on a horizontal shaft driven slowly by a motor. A biofilm develops on the surface of the discs which dip into the sewage. As they turn, the biofilm is exposed to air, providing oxygen for aerobic degradation of the sewage.
Pro:
• Tried and tested.
Cons:
• Some mechanical parts are specific to unit.

Rotary biological contactor

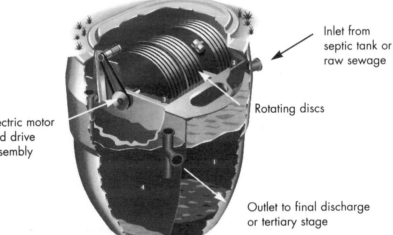

Inlet from
septic tank or
raw sewage

Rotating discs

Electric motor
and drive
assembly

Outlet to final discharge
or tertiary stage

Figure 3.6.1.a. Photograph of a municipal scale rotary biological contactor
(installed above surface).
Figure 3.6.1.b. Cutaway of a rotary biological contactor (installed below
surface) (courtesy of Klargester Environmental Engineering Ltd.).

─────────*Recirculating biological filter*─────────

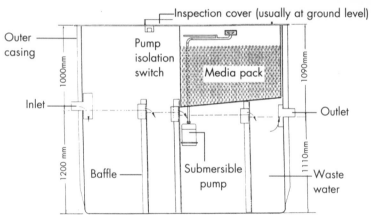

Figure 3.6.2.a. Photograph of a (recently installed) recirculating biological filter.
Figure 3.6.2.b. Cross-section of a recirculating biological filter (courtesy of
Burnham Environmental Services).

6.2 Recirculating biological filters

These units are similar in concept to percolating filters except
that they employ a lightweight plastic matrix housed in a plastic
casing. Effluent is re-circulated over the matrix by electric pump so
no fall is required and the unit can be made smaller than the
equivalent percolating filter. Some designs use a conventional

submersible pump and others use bubble lift pumps with an air compressor (Fig. 3.6.2) but the principle is the same.

Pro:
- Only mechanical part is pump, which is reliable and a standard item.

Con:
- Distribution channels need regular cleaning on some designs.

6.3 Submerged aerated biological filters

This approach involves a process that is a hybridisation of recirculating percolating filters and activated sludge (see 6.4 below). The units include a biological filter through which effluent passes and air is bubbled (Fig. 6.3), usually via a compressed air pump. This is intended to improve efficiency over related approaches.

Pro:
- Increased efficiency (per unit volume).

Con:
- Relatively expensive to operate, because more power needed.

6.4 Activated sludge package plants

These units make use of variations on processes commonly used in large scale municipal treatment works. The small package versions usually involve bubbling air through the incoming sewage. The oxygen is rapidly used to degrade organic matter and this process creates a slurry which contains microorganisms in the most rapid phase of growth, and thus ideal for sewage breakdown. The slurry is allowed to settle, separating the active microbes as sludge from the comparatively clean effluent, which can be removed for further treatment or discharge. In traditional activated sludge systems, a proportion of this sludge is returned to seed the incoming sewage, hence 'activated sludge'. The remaining sludge accumulates and must eventually be removed.

There are several variations on this theme. Some packages involve two or three chambers for aeration and settlement, with sludge recirculation. Others — known as sequencing batch reactors (SBR) — conduct the whole process in a single chamber by temporarily switching off the aeration device to allow settling, then drawing off the liquid for discharge. Sludge remains in the vessel

———Submerged aerated biological filter———

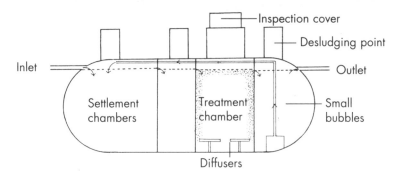

Figure 3.6.3.a. A submerged aerated biological filter (not installed.)
Figure 3.6.3.b. Cross-section of a submerged aerated biological filter (courtesy of Burnham Environmental Services).

ready for the next batch of sewage. The Bio-Bubble SBR (Fig. 3.6.4) achieves high effluent standards with relatively low sludge production, and electricity use by oxygenating only at set periods when required. Most other package plants use electricity on a continuous basis.

Bio-Bubble

Pump and
water level
controls

Figure 3.6.4.a An activated sludge package plant of the SBR type, the 'Bio-Bubble'.

Figure 3.6.4.b. Cutaway drawing of the Bio-Bubble (courtesy of Ekora Products).

Pro:
* Some units aerobically digest the primary sludge.

Other Comments:
* Performance varies between designs from poor to excellent
* Retrofit units available to fit in septic tanks.

7. Vertical Flow Reed Beds

Vertical flow reed beds (Fig. 3.7) are usually preceded by some form of primary treatment, although some have been built to receive raw sewage. Each bed resembles a percolating filter except that it has a layer of sand on top and is planted with aquatic plants, usually the common reed (*Phragmites australis*). The wastewater is introduced in such a way as to cover the surface of the bed and percolate down through the sand and gravel matrix and out at the

Vertical flow reed bed

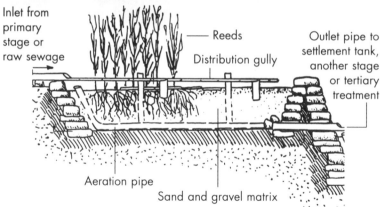

Inlet from primary stage or raw sewage

Reeds

Distribution gully

Outlet pipe to settlement tank, another stage or tertiary treatment

Aeration pipe

Sand and gravel matrix

Figure 3.7.a. Photograph of a vertical flow reed bed.
Figure 3.7.b. Cross-section of a vertical flow reed bed.

base. Intermittent dosing of the bed by pump or flushing device improves distribution and aerates the sand layer by the 'piston effect' as the dose of sewage passes through the bed. As with percolating filters, secondary humus solids are generated and these are usually removed by a humus tank, another vertical flow reed bed or a horizontal flow reed bed.

The sand provides physical filtration as well as an active

biological layer and keeps the bed moist during long periods of rest, an advantage where use is intermittent.

Beds have been built using live willow structures and an organic matrix such as tree bark or mature compost and this offers an even more low cost, ecologically acceptable solution in situations where complete containment is not crucial.

Pros:
- High levels of treatment possible
- DIY possible, which can be very economical
- Needs no power if a gradient is available
- Can be very attractive
- Generates interest, enthusiasm and awareness of sewage
- Maintenance is technically simple
- Biologically complex and robust
- Failure tends to be gradual
- Will work fine before plants are established.

Cons:
- Requires a fall of at least 1.5m to provide good treatment
- Requires more space than conventional systems
- High cost unless DIY
- Often seen wrongly as a green panacea
- Sensitive to hydraulic overloading.

Other Comments:
- Seek advice before DIY, see Resource Guide for courses and advisors
- Sand grading and bed sizing are critical to avoid blockage
- Often two stages, followed by a horizontal flow reed bed
- Requires awareness similar to gardening.

8. Horizontal Flow Reed Beds

Details vary, but there are two main types, subsurface flow and overland flow. The former is more usual in this country, although some have blocked and so have been neatly renamed as overland flow beds! Here we will describe the subsurface flow bed (Fig. 3.8) in which sewage flows horizontally through the gravel or, sometimes, soil. The arrangement can be likened to a bath, filled with gravel and planted with aquatic plants. As you top up the bath, water overflows at the far end. Thus, a depth of water of some

——Box 3.1. So what do the plants do?——

Whilst there is still some difference in opinion we offer the following suggestion as to the function of reeds in reed beds. (Where it is specific to one or the other we indicate VF for vertical flow and HF for horizontal flow.)

Aquatic plants DO:
- Provide beauty, making people more likely to care for the system.
- Blow in the wind, opening up the sand surface of the bed (VF).
- Insulate the bed, providing wind and frost protection.
- Transport air to their roots, which may locally enhance treatment.
- Evapotranspire, so helping (VF) bed regeneration when resting.
- Reduce growth of weeds, i.e. plants that may be less beneficial than reeds.
- Encourage worm activity (VF), increasing surface permeability.
- Increase the C:N ratio of surface film, so accelerating composting (VF).
- Stabilise bed surface (VF).
- Support larger densities of beneficial bacteria than does the surrounding matrix, which may be significant.
- Release selective biocidal compounds, killing harmful microbes, although the significance of this may be small.
- Provide physical filtration and electrostatic attraction of small particles (HF).
- Provide a habitat for microorganisms and larger consumer organisms.
- Take up some heavy metals (HF).

Aquatic plants DO NOT:
- Provide net oxygenation of wastewater (unless already well treated).
- Increase hydraulic flow, due to dead and decaying rhizomes.
- Take up a significant proportion of the dissolved nutrients from the wastewater (in the cool UK climate).
- 'Eat sewage'.

30-50 cm is maintained in the bed, unlike vertical flow beds which are free-draining, with the plug removed. This means less oxygen is available for aerobic treatment. The lower levels of oxygen create ideal conditions for nitrogen removal (cf. page 82).

Whilst they are occasionally used for secondary treatment of sewage, the presence of high levels of organic matter, the low levels of oxygen, and the tendency to block make horizontal flow reed

Horizontal flow reed bed

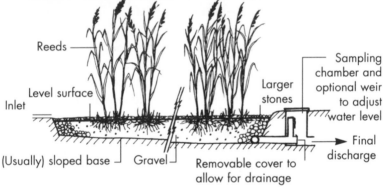

Figure 3.8.a. A horizontal flow reed bed at Newport, Shropshire (4,000 pop.).
Figure 3.8.b. Cross-section of a horizontal flow reed bed.

beds better suited to tertiary treatment, where they do an excellent job removing fine particles of organic matter that are too small to be removed in a settlement tank. Adequate settlement before the horizontal flow bed will extend the bed's life.

Pros:
- Hundreds of horizontal flow reed beds are now in operation in the UK
- Becoming established technology for small and large scale

- Often low cost
- Natural looking
- Need almost no fall
- Provides buffer before the discharge
- Good pathogen removal due to die off and predation
- Minimal maintenance
- Can use a wide range of water plants
- Robust.

Other Comments:
- First UK beds installed in 1986
- Requires about 1 m^2/person for tertiary stage
- Recommended as a tertiary treatment stage
- Not a replacement for secondary treatment systems in our climate
- The role of reeds has been overstated.

9. Solar Ponds

These are also known as waste stabilisation ponds, settlement ponds, lagoons, or sewage ponds. Original installations were in hot countries with a small anaerobic pond at the start, followed by larger aerobic ponds. Because of this tropical origin, any plants which colonised the pond edges were removed, as their stems were insect breeding sites. However, pond systems are now well established as having a role in cooler climes with thousands of such systems long established in the USA and northern Europe. In the UK, recent practice has seen many ponds deliberately seeded with a wide range of aquatic plants (Fig. 3.9), often in tandem with reed beds, making the systems places of great beauty.

Oxygen for the treatment organisms is provided by diffusion from the air over the large surface and by a symbiosis with photosynthesising algae. Although a large surface area is required to ensure sufficient treatment, smaller versions of these systems have been made possible by pumping the water or by using wind powered mixing devices. Especially for small populations and garden installations, many of these ponds have used Flowforms, a particular type of aeration device, described in chapter seven.

Due to their great volume, they can absorb abuse quite well. Unless there are leaks, ponds rarely fail.

Solar pond

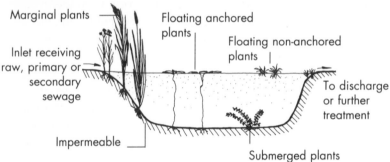

Figure 3.9.a. A solar pond with flowform cascade (recently installed).
Figure 3.9.b. Cross-section of a solar pond.

Pros:
- Robust
- Can provide primary, secondary and tertiary treatment
- Resistant to temporary organic and hydraulic overload
- Can be beautiful
- Pathogen removal can be excellent
- Sludge removal is very infrequent
- May not need liner if clay is present

• DIY possible.

Cons:

• Require large area (approx 10–20 m²/person)
• Occasional odours can be a problem if early stages are not aerated
• Requires power if aerated
• Effluent may contain high levels of algae
• Sludge removal may be difficult
• Expensive for smaller systems
• Needs special health and safety considerations.

10. Leachfields

A leachfield is used as the last part of a treatment system. It is usually preceded by a septic tank and this combination is often referred to as a 'septic tank system'. A leachfield is a series of perforated pipes, surrounded by gravel, that run in underground trenches (Fig. 3.10). With a well designed leachfield in suitable soil, the wastewater is thoroughly cleaned within about a metre of travel through the soil.

In areas with very porous soils, a simple pit full of rocks is often used to receive the wastewater. These 'soakaways ' or 'leach pits' do not ensure passage of water through a sufficient area of soil and so treatment is much reduced. It is arguable that such soakaways should be prohibited because the untreated wastewater can potentially find its way into a drinking water supply.

Failure of the leachfield usually shows as a wet smelly patch on the lawn or when the tank overflows (check for inlet blockage first). This may be caused by long term accumulation of solids or 'sewage sickness', in which case the best solution is to dig a new half-size leachfield away from the old one. This can be used whilst the original field rests and regains its permeability. The two fields can then be alternated on a yearly basis. If the blockage was due to the discharge of gross solids, for example caused by overdue sludge removal or a broken dip pipe (see septic tanks, 3.2 above), then it would be worth having the leachfield pressure-jetted by a contractor once the cause has been cured. If it works this is the cheapest solution.

When installing a new leachfield there are several things that

Leachfield

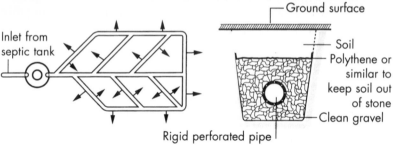

Figure 3.10.a. Photograph of a leachfield (installed in the foreground).
Figure 3.10.b. Plan view of herringbone leachfield used where single pipe would be too long.
Figure 3.10.c. Cross-section of a leachfield.

---

can be done to improve performance and longevity. We recommend our booklet *Septic Tanks: an Overview* (see Resource Guide).

Pros:
- First choice for on-site sewage disposal system
- Very well established
- Provides treatment and disposal
- May require a large area but this can be under a lawn, etc.
- No odour when properly installed

- Invisible
- Excellent treatment when correctly installed in appropriate situation
- Little or no maintenance
- Lowest cost secondary treatment
- Natural treatment in its simplest and most efficient form.

Cons:

- Rather unglamorous
- Fissures in the ground or land drains can allow untreated effluent to reach a watercourse or well
- Ground must be suitable and the winter water table over 1m below the trench bottom
- Water recovery difficult unless crops are grown in leachfield.

Other Comments:

- An old existing leachfield may not cope with high volume modern water usage.

11. Willows and Trenches

When sewage has been treated to a sufficiently high standard one may wish to discharge the effluent to the surface of the soil as an irrigant. For the sewage this is a very useful final 'polish', since the topsoil is even more efficient than subsoil at 'absorbing' nutrients and the final suspended matter. For the soil, it is a source of both moisture and nutrients, and allows the growth of a crop. The authors' experience is only of growing trees — mainly willows, growing between shallow irrigation channels (Fig. 3.11; see chapter seven for details) — but most plants will thrive.

Pros:

- Provides tertiary treatment and often disposal to ground
- Produces a useful crop
- Can be beautiful
- Good wildlife habitat
- Ideal DIY.

Cons:

- Can be a dull monoculture
- Requires a large area of suitable land
- Possible environmental health considerations.

Willow and trench

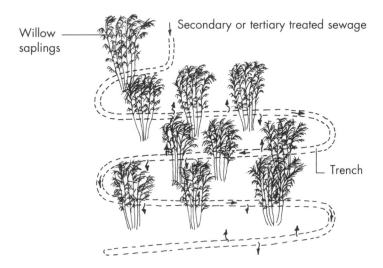

Willow saplings

Secondary or tertiary treated sewage

Trench

Figure 3.11.a. Photograph of a willow and trench treatment stage (with sheer mulch).

Figure 3.11.b. Bird's eye view of a willow and trench treatment stage.

Other Comments:
• Needs weed and possibly pest control if harvest is for craft use
• Yield increased by nutrients but may be poor quality for basketry
• Usually, discharge standard must be met before this stage
• Will not dry up wet ground in winter.

12. Living Machines

This name, coined by Ocean Arks International (an organisation led by Dr. John Todd, the main developer of this approach), describes artificial ecosystems, constructed in a carefully formalised manner. Their design is based on a number of principles intended to maximise the similarity of the constructed ecosystem to its counterpart in nature. A key feature is the seeding of the system with selected organisms, minerals and other materials. The aim is to lead to a self-designing dynamic equilibrium, capable of utilising all the sewage (or other waste, including solid material, or industrial waste) such that virtually *no* contaminants remain in the water. If there is significant residual contamination this is regarded as incomplete design and further fine tuning is made.

Most Living Machines are industrial treatment systems. However, there are also many used to treat domestic sewage at a small community scale and even for single households. The biological fluidised bed (Fig. 3.12.b), for example, is a technology that can be installed as part of a Living Machine, on a large or household scale. The enormous surface area of the plant roots involved are claimed to provide an effective cleaning process.

Full information can be obtained from Living Technologies, UK, or Watershed (see Resource Guide).

Pros:
• Visually interesting
• Educationally valuable, because many organism interactions are observable
• High levels of treatment possible.

Cons:
• Expensive

——————————*Living machines*——————————

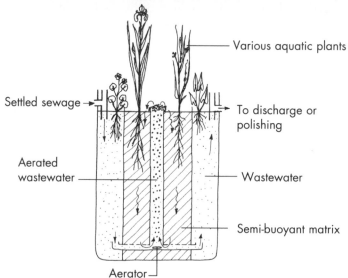

Figure 3.12.a. A 'Living Machine' in a greenhouse, Providence, Rhode Island, USA.

Figure 3.12.b. Cross-section of a biological fluidised bed.

- Not well established in the UK
- Usually require a lot of energy
- Require close management.

Other Comments:
- More appropriate to treatment of complex industrial waste, rather than domestic sewage
- A concept and design philosophy rather than a specific technology
- Has gained a 'green' image.

If it ain't broke don't fix it
Upgrading your existing sewage treatment system

It is not unheard of for people, perhaps bitten by the reed bed bug, to rip out intact but underachieving sewage treatment systems, and replace them with a sexy new reed bed. This is, after all, how two of the authors ended up in their present line of work. In hindsight, knowing a little more than we did then, we can see that we could have saved a lot of money, time and hassle by fixing what we already had rather than ripping it out.

The offending sewage system was a percolating filter that was failing its consent on BOD and suspended solids. The first mistake we made was not to realise that the samples the NRA inspector was taking were not wholly sewage; the outlet pipe was broken, so it acted as a land drain collecting mud and dissolved cow pat from the field it passed through. Since this was not discovered until we had served our sewage apprenticeship, we will never know how badly the original plant was actually working but it is very likely that it could have been brought up to standard relatively simply (Fig. 3.13 overleaf).

The two main weaknesses of the old filter were that it received rainwater from a roof and courtyard and that the humus tank was undersized. The first of these had to be rectified before the reed bed was built anyway, and the second could have been fixed by the addition of an extra tank. We would then have had a reasonable system that probably would have met the required legal standards (with a little luck).

—————Upgrading a sewage treatment system—————

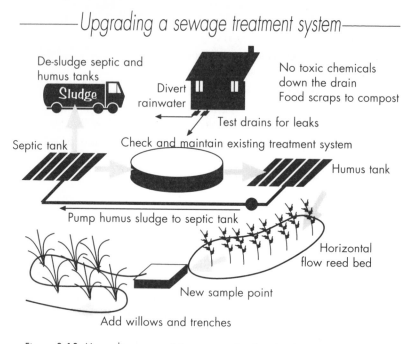

Figure 3.13. Upgrading your existing sewage treatment system.

The Horizontal Flow Reed Bed Fix

The main weakness of trickling filters, RBCs and indeed most conventional biological treatment systems, is that they tend not to be very good at removing the finest suspended solids and their associated organic matter, and indeed they add some secondary solids of their own making. A fairly simple fix is to add a horizontal flow reed bed on to the end of the existing system. Sizing is not too critical, but 1m^2/person is a good rule of thumb for a gravel-filled bed, with perhaps a minimum area of 6m^2. The larger the bed, the longer it will take to block with humus solids. Such a bed will give instant results when tacked on to a system with an undersized humus tank, but is a poor substitute for adequate settlement — a tank is far easier to empty than to clean a clogged bed.

A reed bed, at this scale, should be 400mm deep and three to four times longer than it is wide. You can use a pond liner to keep

Box 3.2. Before Upgrading — Checklist

• Check roof and other rain water does not enter system.

• Check drains for leaks after heavy rain.

• Check for dripping taps and other water wastage that might overload the system.

• Check septic/settlement tanks for broken dip pipes and sludge level.

• Check biological treatment plant for correct function and service as recommended by supplier.

---

reeds and effluent in, and weed roots, surface water and soil particles out. The gravel should be of uniform grade, for example 20mm diameter local washed stone or crushed rock.

Plant the bed with local water plants, most of which grow very easily from sections of rhizome. The most vigorous will quickly dominate your bed. The common reed, *Phragmites australis*) (syn *P. communis*), may be slightly better at treating sewage and it stays standing over winter.

You could also discharge to land or willows as described above and in chapter seven.

The moral of this cautionary take is not to rush into ripping out an existing system even if it is failing. First evaluate the problem (see Box 3.2), aided by your new-found understanding and enthusiasm for sewage treatment. Then weigh up the pros and cons of the various solutions and make an informed decision. You may find a suitable fix for your existing system, or you may discover that your treatment plant is near the end of its useful life, uses large amounts of electricity, and that another of the systems described above is just the thing.

Whilst detailed design and troubleshooting are beyond the scope of this introductory book, it should give you the tools to know if your existing treatment plant is likely to be worth saving.

Summary

On-site treatment of sewage can be achieved by rationally combining any of a wide variety of methods. Both conventional and 'alternative' methods have appropriate application, no single approach being suitable in all situations.

The upgrading of an existing system that is apparently under-performing may well be best served by a combination of modified water use, repair of the system and/or the addition of a single treatment element, rather than its replacement with a whole new treatment system.

Chapter Four
Monitoring the Success of Sewage Treatment

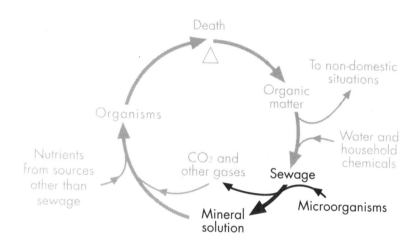

So far we have discussed the context, the processes and the hardware for on-site sewage treatment. But, whether you choose to upgrade an existing system or to install a new one, or if you simply want to assess how an existing system is performing, some method of monitoring treatment success is necessary.

This chapter deals with some methods and attempts to explain what the results of such approaches really mean:

1. Monitoring methods
2. Regulators and regulations.

Monitoring Methods

We can identify four approaches to water quality assessment, of increasing sophistication:

1. The jam-jar method
2. The turbidity tube
3. Biotic indices
4. Biochemical tests.

The Jam-jar Method

A simple way of checking whether your system is functioning is to obtain a jam-jar of the effluent and observe and smell the contents (Fig. 2.2). From this you will get a fairly good and instant bit of feedback which will become more and more reliable as your experience grows. The colour will let you know whether there are algae present, and grit and pebbles will be readily apparent. The cloudiness is an indicator of both suspended solids and BOD. However, the jam-jar technique is subjective and not suitable for gathering data you can compare from day to day.

The Turbidity Tube

A simple step towards quantifying such monitoring is the turbidity tube (Fig. 4.1) — a long thin transparent tube with calibrations down its length and a black cross on the bottom of the tube. Look down the cylinder to the cross and pour in sewage until you can no longer see the cross. Then read off the height of the liquid. That is the turbidity reading. A long transparent column of sewage (before obscuring the cross) indicates clean water; a shallow depth indicates dirty water. The figures obtained from one reading can be compared with those from others. But the method is still subjective;

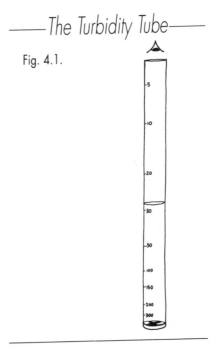

——The Turbidity Tube——

Fig. 4.1.

different people, and/or light conditions yield poorly correlating results.

The beauty of the above methods is their simplicity in providing a rough guide to water quality. However, they suffer from providing only a small part of the picture and from lack of comparability. In particular, the methods tell us nothing about how the organisms encountering such water will be affected. The most direct method of investigating this is quite simply to observe the behaviour of living organisms in contact with the discharged water.

One of the main reasons that we treat sewage is to protect the water-course into which the sewage is discharged, so that 'higher' forms of life (such as fish) will be able to thrive in the water. Rearranging this line of reasoning, we should get an idea of the degree of health of a watercourse by looking at the creatures thriving there.

It is relatively easy to become familiar with what is living in the water into which you are proposing to discharge treated sewage, by sitting still for some time and observing the plants and animals — snails, larvae, newts, perhaps even fish — living there. A magnifying glass and a field guide can assist you. All those critters are at your mercy.

Biotic Indices

By careful study it has been possible to gather enough information about the various life forms such that the presence or absence of particular species in an environment is indicative of the life-supporting capacity of that niche. This compilation of information has led to lists of organisms alongside their ecological significance. A table of such information is known as a biotic index.

The advantage of using a biotic index, rather than biochemical methods (see below), for water quality assessment is that aquatic organisms are *continuous indicators* of water quality. These organisms are affected by discharges whether they occur when the Environment Agency pollution control officer sticks their sample bottle under the pipe or whether there just happens to be a little discharge of highly contaminated effluent in the middle of the night. Theoretically the EA could look at the creatures in a

GROUP	FAMILIES	SCORE
Mayflies	Siphlonuridae, Heptageniidae, Leptophlebiidae, Ephemerellidae, Potamanthidae, Ephemereidae	10
Stoneflies	Taeniopterygidae, Leuctridae, Capniidae, Perlodidae, Perlidae, Chloroperlidae	10
River Bug	Aphelocheiridae	10
Caddis	Phryganeidae, Molannidae, Beraeidae, Odontoceridae, Leptoceridae, Goeridae, Lepidostomatidae, Brachycentridae, Sericostomatidae	10
Crayfish	Astacidae	8
Dragonflies	Lestidae, Agriidae, Gomphidae, Cordulegasteridae, Aeshnidae, Corduliidae, Libellulidae	8
Mayflies	Caenidae	7
Stoneflies	Nemouridae	7
Caddis	Rhyacophilidae, Polycontropodidae, Limnephilidae	7
Snails	Neritidae, Viviparidae, Ancylidae	6
Caddis	Hydroptilidae	6
Mussels	Unionidae	6
Shrimps	Corophiidae, Gammaridae	6
Dragonfiles	Platycnemididae, Coenagriidae	6
Bugs	Mesoveliidae, Hydrometridae, Gerridae, Nepidae, Naucoridae, Notonectidae, Pleidae, Corixidae	5
Beetles	Haliplidae, Hygrobiidae, Dytiscidae, Gyrinidae, Hydrophilidae, Clambidae, Helodidae, Dryopidae, Elmidae, Chrysomelidae, Curculionidae	5
Caddis	Hydropsychidae	5
Craneflies/ Blackflies	Tipulidae, Simuliidae	5
Flatworms	Planariidae, Dendrocoelidae	5
Mayflies	Baetidae	4
Alderflies	Sialidae	4
Leeches	Piscicolidae	4
Snails	Valvatidae, Hydrobiidae, Lymnaeidae, Physidae, Planorbidae	3
Cockles	Sphaeriidae	3
Leeches	Glossiphoniidae, Hirudidae, Erpobdellidae	3
Hog louse	Asellidae	3
Midges	Chironomidae	2
Worms	Oligochaeta (whole class)	1

Figure 4.2. The Biological Monitoring Working Party biotic index.

Living Determinands

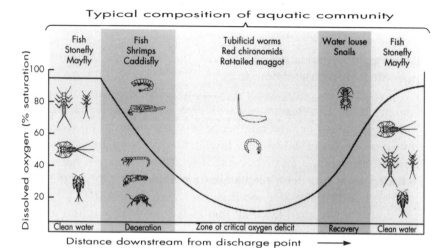

Fig. 4.3. Invertebrates as an indication of water quality either side of a sewage discharge point. (After Horan - see Resource Guide.)

receiving water and base their decision on how much and what quality of effluent could be discharged without affecting the water's ability to maintain those populations.

There have been several attempts to formalise this general concept. The one we shall mention here is the BMWP system (Fig. 4.2). The Biological Monitoring Working Party was set up by the Department of Environment and National Water Council to make a score card (a 'green gauge') for the various invertebrates which might be found in freshwater habitats. These invertebrates are characterised in Fig. 4.3, which shows the typical effect of a sewage discharge on a clean stream in terms of the oxygen level and the range of invertebrates living there. Thus, if river bugs (*Aphelocheiridae*) and cray fish (*Astacidae*) are in the water, it is probably fairly high quality but if there are only midge larvae (*Chironomidae*) and worms (*Oligochaeta*), you might think twice about having a long cool drink from the stream.

Invertebrates are used to judge the quality of water for a

number of reasons: they are a diverse group that are practically ubiquitous in freshwater; they tend to stay put, which means the survey tends to be a fair reflection of what happens in the area and makes performing and analysing the surveys relatively cheap; and, because they are relatively long-lived, they reflect the standard of the water over a useful time span.

The weakness of most scoring systems is that they are not really standardised. To achieve standardisation would involve carefully recording the variety and number of creatures, taking into account the type of water body (e.g. lowland, clay pond or highland sandstone brook), and choosing the different micro-habitats (shaded or in full light, planted or unplanted, etc.) to sample at various points in the year and then averaging the results.

However, we shall leave all that to the professionals and give you a fairly simple method and a table for scoring. The method is known as the 'kick sweep sample'. One places a long-handled net (mesh size about 0.5mm, rigid frame) into the bank of the pond, river or stream while a friend holds a stopwatch. The best populated site is likely to be where there is some mud and shingle with plants rooted in them. For a given time (a minute is quite tiring) you thrust the net vigorously into the bank and lift up the material into the water. Repeat the process again and again until the timekeeper says stop. Then empty the muck, weeds, creatures, and so on from the net into a container, add some water, and take the container back to a place where the contents can be scrutinised beneath a lens.

A good field guide to invertebrates should be consulted, with care; a lot of these creatures look very similar to each other. After the critters are isolated and identified, they should be returned to the watercourse if possible.

So you have a table of creatures and you have used your field guide to identify which family they belong to. Now add up your total to get your BMWP score. What did you score? 250? Incredible! 200 would be extraordinary.

The qualitative score alone (i.e. not taking the quantity of each invertebrate into account) can now be compared to the RIVPACS score (River Invertebrate Prediction and Classification System). RIVPACS takes into account the width and depth of the water body, the altitude and distance from the source, the underlying substrates, the flow and slope of the river, and the calcium carbonate content of the water.

The RIVPACS score (biotic index) gives the best possible score for the characteristics of the watercourse, and the BMWP score gives the actual score based on your findings. The RIVPACS system can be found in a book called *The New Rivers and Wildlife Handbook* (ISBN 9-780903-138703). If you divide the latter by the former (the actual by the potential maximum), you get the Environmental Quality Index (EQI). An EQI approaching one indicates there is no stress on the river/pond/stream and that all the invertebrates one would expect in such conditions are actually there. The lower the score, the greater the stress of the stream. EQIs are potentially comparable to the EA's (Environment Agency's — see Regulators and Regulations, below) river classification system ratings but this, as far as we are aware, has not been formalised. Perhaps one day people will be allowed to discharge used water only if *Siphlonuridae* (a mayfly family) larvae are demonstrably still able to thrive in the receiving water!

Biochemical Tests

The methods described in the preceding three sections are limited by their lack of reproducibility and the difficulty of valid comparison between different tests at different times and places. When setting standards that the public are asked to achieve by law, the regulatory authorities are obliged to utilise methods that do not suffer from these limitations. Scientific rigour is required, as far as is possible in such a variable subject as sewage analysis. For this, specific analytical tests (usually, but not always, needing specialist training and expensive equipment) have been devised, each measuring a different characteristic — 'determinand' — of the wastewater. In order fully to understand sewage treatment, such that you are in a position to design your own system or make the best of upgrading an existing system, you would do well to arm yourself with a basic knowledge of these determinands.

This is a somewhat technical section but nonetheless important when it comes to talking the same language as the regulatory authorities. It is arranged as follows:

———Box 4.1. Primary and Secondary Solids———

Sewage that has had nothing done to it is called unsettled or raw sewage. It contains a certain amount of material that could be intercepted in a laboratory filter and, therefore, gives a suspended solids reading. In the process of being treated, these lumps — ' primary solids ' — are settled out of the flow of liquid or transformed and dissolved in the liquid. Thus the original SS gradually diminishes. However, the proliferation of mortal microorganisms in sewage inevitably means lots of micro-carcasses. These are susceptible to filtration and so can also register as suspended solids. These are generated in the sewage treatment process (rather than being present in the raw influent) and are distinguished from the primary solids by being named 'secondary solids'. UK law requires that the consent for suspended solids is achieved regardless of whether the solids are primary or secondary.

---

1. The major determinands —SS and BOD
2. Other determinands — nitrogen, phosphorus, sulphur, pathogens
3. Interpreting biochemical analysis data.

The Major Determinands —SS and BOD

The regulatory authorities use two main determinands to set discharge standards to be achieved by small sewage treatment systems. Many other determinands exist that are considered to be of less importance (at the small scale) with respect to the health of natural water bodies (see Other Determinands, below).

Suspended solids (SS) Let us start with the simplest to understand — suspended solids or SS (pronounced 'ess - ess ' rather than as the sound of gas escaping). It is a quick and cheap measure of the amount of solid material in the water.

If you were to fill a jar with a litre of water from your sewage outfall and then take it to a laboratory, the laboratory technicians would pass the sample through a filter of standard pore size and known weight. They would carefully heat the wet filter to drive off the moisture, and then re-weigh the filter. The difference between this measured weight and the weight of the clean filter is the weight of the suspended solids in one litre of effluent. SS is usually cited in milligrams per litre (mg/l).

Suspended solids create problems in watercourses. Depending

Suspended solids measurement

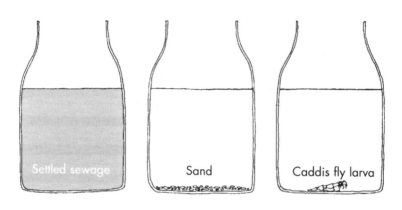

Figure 4.4. Water-borne solids of differing character but giving the same SS measurement.

---

on their size, concentration and quantity, they can block gills, obscure light, hit fish on the back of the head, or divert the flow of the stream.

Roughly 60% of the organic load of domestic sewage is in the form of lumps. Thus, a high SS is a good indication that there is a lot of organic stuff in there. However, SS alone is not sufficient to indicate that there is a pollution problem, since it includes grit and other biochemically inert particles (see Fig. 4.4). Therefore, other tests are needed that, when viewed in combination with SS, can reveal more about the litre of water.

Biochemical Oxygen Demand (BOD) The oxygen that microorganisms require in order to break down organic matter is called the biochemical oxygen demand. This mouthful is commonly referred to as the BOD (pronounced 'bee-oh-dee ').

BOD is measured in milligrams of oxygen removed per litre of water over a certain period of time. The time element is important. For example, consider a tree. A tree has a huge BOD. The amount of oxygen required to digest an old oak tree that has fallen in a stream is enormous. But it will take years for all that digestion to take place, and the demand for oxygen by the microorganisms will be spread out over those years. In any given period of time the

─────────── Box 4.2. Five Days ───────────

When the decisions about standardised tests were being made it was agreed to make the BOD incubation last for 5 days since this was calculated as about the average time for sewage to reach the mouth of the average British river. It also gave time for fairly complete degradation of the carbonaceous matter without too much oxygen used for nitrogen degradation in domestic sewage. Any shorter and the degradation would have a long way to go and any longer would not reveal much more about the samples. In a few countries this time is increased to seven days (fitting in better with the working week) and the paperwork shows BOD_7, rather than BOD_5.

oxygen removed from the water will be negligible compared to what is available in the flowing water.

Contrast this to rapidly decaying organic matter such as an ox-pat. Suppose an ox was fording a stream and chose that moment to exercise its urge to defecate. The microorganisms would get to work very rapidly but they would be finished very quickly. During that short period of time, Oxford would be full of lower organisms. (This brings to mind a definition of Oxford and Cambridge, once mumbled by a person who little values academic learning: "Oxford and Cambridge — the only two towns where everyone knows how to spell 'diarrhoea'.")

In terms of the stream's ability to sustain higher organisms, the ox-pat is a greater challenge than the tree, even though the total oxygen requirement is less. Therefore, the figure of BOD set by the regulatory authorities usually has a little number after it, and usually that figure is a 5; hence BOD_5. This means that the amount of oxygen required by the degrading organisms is measured over five days in the laboratory incubator and is, therefore, a rate of oxygen utilisation, rather than a total. So the units for BOD should be 'mg O_2/litre/120 hours'.

Even worse than an ox-pat in a stream is a sewage discharge that continues day and night throughout the year. If salmon returning to spawning grounds encounter a cow pat, they can loiter some distance downstream until the trouble is digested and dispersed. If they encounter the continuous discharge of a sewage outfall or a farm yard, the salmon will have to wait until the house

————Box 4.3. Other Tests Related to BOD————

There are several other tests for the oxygen demand of a discharge, that are related to but significantly different from BOD. The most often seen is COD or chemical oxygen demand. This is useful when the test sample contains compounds that are not degradable by microorganisms, or not biologically degraded within the five-day incubation period. COD usually gives a higher figure than BOD because it includes all the material oxidised in the BOD test plus a host of other compounds. TOC (total organic carbon) gives an indication of the ability of the liquid to burn — an indication of the total organic and other combustible matter present. Like COD, this gives no indication of the source or rate at which the demand is required, so does not distinguish between the tree, the cow pat, or even a fuel spill. The NRA was keen to introduce this determinand since it is quick and cheap and the hope was that if BOD and TOC were established for a given discharge the ratio between the two could be calculated. In future the simpler TOC test would then be a sufficient indication of the BOD.

---

becomes derelict or the subsidies are removed from milk production. Experience shows that salmon do not wait that long.

BOD is also dependent on temperature. The organisms degrading either the tree or cow pat are much more enthusiastic about their task when the stream is flowing with warm water, than when it is freezing. Therefore, the BOD is measured at a standard temperature (20°C) to make comparisons meaningful.

Finally, you may see BOD figures on technical forms cited as BOD_5 + ATU. ATU (allylthiourea) is a chemical added to inhibit another pathway of degradation that also requires oxygen ('nitrification' — see the discussion below).

To simplify further — and this is all you really need to grasp — big BOD is bad, little BOD is good. The same is true for SS. If you return the water at lower numbers than the levels set by the authorities, you will not be asked to explain yourself, improve your system or pay a fine.

Why is oxygen demanded? It can be very helpful in refining elements of the design of a sewage system, and in becoming a creative designer for treatment of all kinds of effluents, to know where the demand for oxygen, or BOD, is coming from. The

---------------------*Box 4.4. Milk*---------------------

Would you prefer a discharge of milk or of hydrochloric acid into your favourite trout stream? If one were simply to consider BOD one would in fact prefer the acid since bacteria do not thrive in it and thus they would demand no oxygen. Milk, on the other hand, is transformed rapidly and profoundly by microorganisms; one only needs to leave a bottle on the window sill for a few warm hours to see that this is so. The microorganisms would consume about 150,000 mg (0.15 kg) of oxygen for every litre of milk they sour, over 5 days at 20°C. Hydrochloric acid is harmful in other ways, creating conditions too acidic for normal biological activity. This shows the importance of analysing a range of parameters — i.e. the 'suite' of determinands — for a sample, if its full pollution potential is to be revealed.

Examples of average BOD_5 in mg/l:

Tertiary treated sewage	2 — 20
Secondary treated sewage	10 — 20
Raw sewage	100 — 400
Farmyard washings	1,000 — 2,000
Vegetable washings	3,000
Cattle slurry	10,000 — 20,000
Silage effluent	12,000 — 80,000
Milk	150,000

majority of microbial activity that contributes to this demand for oxygen is the metabolism of organic matter — which by definition contains carbon. The carbon itself binds to several other chemical elements as well as to itself, and it is the breaking of these bonds that requires oxygen.

An *aide memoire* for the six major chemical elements that make up living tissues is NCHOPS — the chemical symbols for (respectively): nitrogen, carbon, hydrogen, oxygen, phosphorus and sulphur. Combinations of these elements comprise the majority of living matter, along with smaller doses of other elements such as potassium and sodium, and even smaller amounts of trace elements such as zinc and cobalt. Space and degree of relevance force us to limit this discussion of biochemistry to NCHOPS.

In organic matter, these elements are found in various combinations to give fats (mainly carbon and hydrogen), carbohydrates

─────────────Carbofatein Molecule─────────────

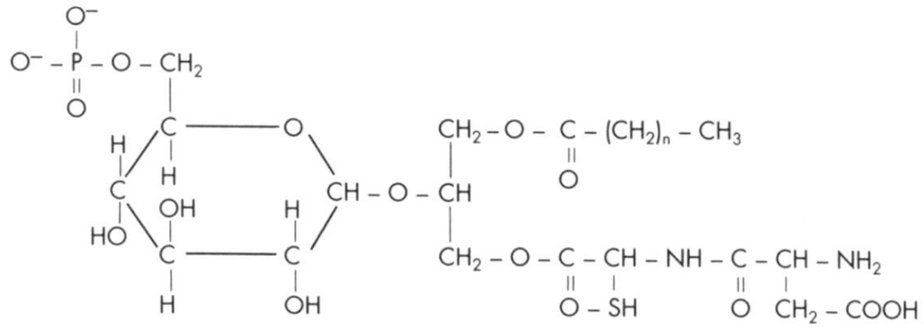

Figure 4.5. A hypothetical organic molecule, carbofatein.

(mainly carbon hydrogen and oxygen) and proteins (mainly carbon, hydrogen, oxygen and nitrogen), plus many other types of molecule. Phosphorus and sulphur are found in lesser amounts in all three categories. For illustrative purposes we could invent a hypothetical hybrid molecule to represent what happens when organic matter decays. Let us call this invention 'carbofatein' (Fig. 4.5).

The overall structure of carbofatein (and real organic molecules) is held together and dominated by long chains of carbon atoms. Biochemists refer to the carbon 'backbone' or the carbon 'skeleton' of a molecule. When a bond linking a carbon atom is broken energy becomes available, which the microorganisms can utilise. Because oxygen can be used to allow this breaking of bonds, a demand for oxygen — the BOD — exists.

As the carbon bonds are severed, and the descending arc of the Big Circle is travelled, the incredibly long molecules that make up cabbages and other organic matter are degraded to smaller organic fragments, which have less energy stored within them. If oxygen is available, it is consumed in the process, being converted to water. The fragments, too, will degrade until they become classified as mineral or inorganic.

Each of the six main elements in organic molecules will eventually arrive at the bottom of the circle in its own way. Carbon will emerge as carbon dioxide eventually and be released to the

—————————Box 4.5. *Goethe 's Bone of*————
Contention, Wöhler 's Mole of Invention

In the middle of the current millennium, as the dogmas of the church crumbled and the search for new certainty in a mysterious world was starting, discussion of scientific matters was still heavily influenced by theological considerations. Human beings were considered to be above the animals, and the difference was even anatomically demonstrated by the absence of the intermaxilliary bone in man which was so obvious in mammals. This particular line of debate was rather set back when Goethe discovered that not only man but woman too does indeed have this bone.

A similar setback was suffered when debaters opined that there are no biochemicals that man could make since only God can make them. Then along came Friedrich Wöhler in 1828 and created urea in a test tube (a 'piece of piss' to today's biochemists), giving a terrific boost to the school in the ascendant which thought that all of creation's secrets lay hidden in the atoms of the elements of chemistry.

---

environment as gas or remain dissolved in the water as carbonic acid. Hydrogen and oxygen are lost for choice as to which elements they will escape with (see Box 2.1).

Other Determinands — nitrogen, phosphorus, sulphur, pathogens.

Nitrogen The sewage industry takes a very great interest in nitrogen and there is a lot of information about the water quality to be gleaned from the measurements of nitrogen in its various forms. As we mentioned, nitrogen is to be found mainly, though not exclusively, in the proteinaceous material of tissues. As this protein is degraded, the nitrogen will follow a well-documented pathway. This starts within the body, and urea is the main form in which N is excreted from our bodies, which will be degraded to ammonia.

Ammonia is simple to measure and is a frequently used determinand partly for that reason. It is also directly toxic to some creatures (young fish especially) and it is important to have a gauge of its concentration for that reason alone. However, for the sewage worker ammonia analysis also lets us know two things.

The first is whether carbon breakdown has proceeded to relative completion. It has been found that in most types of sewage treatment system, the microorganisms that transform ammonia wait until the BOD has fallen to a large extent, before they start their work. In general we can say that if the ammonia concentration has dropped between the inlet and outlet of a stage of a treatment system, then substantial breakdown of organic matter has also occurred (and that can be ascertained even without taking a measurement of BOD).

The second thing which the ammonia reading will indicate is whether there is any oxygen available. The ammonia-transforming bacteria also require oxygen before they start their work. If there is no oxygen available, nitrogen will be preserved in the form of ammonia whatever the BOD.

Assuming that there is oxygen available and carbon bonds are mainly broken, what would happen to the ammonia? If in high concentration, especially if the pH is significantly above neutral, ammonia will come out of solution and be lost as a gas. However, this is not the main route of ammonia loss from domestic sewage. Much more common is that ammonia is oxidised and the nitrogen becomes bound as nitrate, after passing swiftly through an intermediate stage of nitrite. This process is known as 'nitrification'. It is the process which ATU (see BOD, p. 75) inhibits since ATU blocks the action of the nitrifying bacteria. *Nitrosomonas* (and allies) change ammonia to nitrite and *Nitrobacter* (*et al*) take it on from there to create nitrate. This two-step process requires oxygen to be present (about 5 mg for each mg of ammonia which is transformed) and is, therefore, a contributor to BOD unless ATU or another nitrification inhibitor is present. It also requires some inorganic carbon source for the bacteria's cell synthesis. This source is usually carbonic acid (at the rate of about 9 mg for each mg of ammonia transformed).

Nitrifying bacteria also require some heat and do practically nothing in the winter temperatures (<5 °C), which is why most sewage systems return high ammonia figures in the cold. So you can see that for ammonia transformation there are many conditions which need to be right: temperature, low BOD, the presence of oxygen and inorganic carbon sources, and not too much nitrate, ammonia, or ATU.

Assuming, however, that this set of circumstances is met, nitrate is the form in which all nitrogen from the original organic compounds is found at the bottom of the Big Circle in the mineral solution. That is to say that if a sewage works has done this part of the job well it will discharge nitrates. There are of course many problems associated with nitrate production and disposal. But poor treatment by the sewage plant is not usually one of them. Urea discharge is unlikely, ammonia discharge is common and difficult to eliminate entirely, but nitrate discharge indicates that the wider water environment does not have to use up precious oxygen to break down the nitrogenous material. So, what fate could, and indeed sometimes does, await nitrate after discharge?

You will recall that we called the process of conversion of ammonia to nitrate 'nitrification'. The process of degrading or removing nitrate is called 'denitrification' and cannot take place until nitrification has taken place. The chemical formula for nitrate is NO_3^-, indicating that each nitrogen atom is bound with three oxygen atoms. That oxygen can seem mighty attractive to certain bacteria if there is no other free oxygen around. (Conditions where there is no unbound oxygen are known as 'anoxic'.) A gagging microorganism can get to thinking that that nitrogen is too damn greedy for its own good in times of oxygen hardship and better start sharing. In the absence of free oxygen breezing about, this sharing takes place. The nitrate's oxygen is escorted off by the microorganism and the nitrogen has to manage with less — with just two oxygens as NO_2^- (nitrite); as a one-oxygen-molecule (NO, nitric oxide); even sharing with another nitrogen (N_2O, nitrous oxide); or just getting on without oxygen at all as N_2 (nitrogen gas). The latter is by far the most abundant product of denitrification, the others being unstable intermediates. N_2 gas thus leaves the water and joins the huge quantity that already exists as 79% of the air we breathe. It is a totally harmless product of nitrogen metabolism.

A second means of removing the nitrate from solution is by having it taken up into the roots of plants as part of their living tissue or 'biomass'. However, even in reed beds, in our climate, this is a minority route for removal of nitrate from sewage wastewater as compared to what can be achieved by making unbound oxygen scarce. (In warmer climates there is evidence of significant contributions to the removal of nitrate by the uptake into regularly harvested plants.)

Therefore, to assist nitrogen compounds efficiently through their path towards mineral soup you must ensure that your sewage treatment plant *first* allows plenty of air into the water, in order to allow nitrification. After that you have a choice: you can take the water through a low oxygen environment, to allow *de*nitrification; or you can take the water through an aerobic environment in which plants can remove some of the nitrate by root uptake.

Biochemical analyses are used to measure the various nitrogen-containing molecules, either singly or in groups. Note that analytical results usually record the amount of a single element (e.g. N) in a molecule (e.g. NH_3, NO_3^-), in order that the amount of that element converted between one form and another is easy to see from the data. The main nitrogenous determinands are:

Total Kjeldahl nitrogen — TKN (organic-N plus ammoniacal-N)
Ammoniacal nitrogen — NH_3-N, or NH_4^+-N
Nitrite nitrogen — NO_2-N
Nitrate nitrogen — NO_3-N
Total oxidised nitrogen — TON (nitrate-N plus nitrite-N)

It is worth emphasising that an understanding of the nitrogen pathways and the various determinands — as described above — is essential if you are to design a sewage treatment system capable of removing more than just the BOD and SS.

Phosphorus Phosphorus is a fascinating element in biochemistry. The reactions that generate energy in cells all involve compounds containing phosphorus. Half the phosphorus in domestic sewage is from our excrement; the end product of our metabolism. The other half is mainly due to the phosphates that are added to washing powders.

The determinand for phosphorus is usually orthophosphate (usually referred to simply as phosphate — PO_4^{3-}), which is metabolically available phosphorus combined with four atoms of oxygen. Orthophosphate contrasts with pyrophosphate (two P atoms) and polyphosphates (several P atoms).

Removal of phosphate is not simple in a wastewater system. It

—————————— *Box 4.6. Water Softening* ——————

Phosphorus is added to washing powders in order to reduce the influence of calcium and magnesium carbonate in the water, thus softening the water to make the soaps more effective. The irony is that calcium is sometimes added at sewage treatment works to flocculate the phosphorus out again!

is possible to manipulate the amount of oxygen available to the sewage and create an alternation of aerobic and anaerobic conditions, which a bacterium known as *Acinetobacter* can then exploit, thus removing phosphate from the water. However this is so difficult and expensive to achieve, that it really has no place in the systems we might build for ourselves.

A more practicable means of phosphorus removal is by making it stick to something — a process called adsorption. (Adsorption means sticking to a surface, as opposed to *ab*sorption where something is taken into something else.) The main surfaces to which phosphorus tends to stick are rich in iron, aluminium, or calcium. Adsorption is possible when there are lots of stones or soil in the system being used. Clay in particular is full of aluminium and binds phosphate. Such adsorption systems are usually excellent when first used and then become progressively less adept because the phosphate binding sites become occupied. Indeed, with changes in pH the adsorption fluctuates and there can be releases of the previously bound phosphorus.

Some phosphate is also taken up directly into living cells and can be removed from the water by removing the organisms, either as sludge or by harvesting plants. In municipal sewage treatment systems, if removal is required, phosphorus is bound to some chemical that brings it out of solution and makes it susceptible to gravity — a two stage process of flocculation and settlement. The disposal of this sludge then becomes the issue.

Phosphorus must be removed from bodies of water because it is the nutrient most critical to eutrophication — over-richness of nutrients and thus life. The growth of algae in the receiving water is always limited by the lack of one nutrient or another. Often, phosphorus is that limiting nutrient and when it is supplied the algae grow in abundance, blocking light, so preventing

Box 4.7. Best Laid Plans

Byron's Bay, in Australia, is a big resort for bronzing bodies and catching the surf. To protect the tourist industry it is important to keep the coastal waters clean and attractive. A big wetlands system has been added to the municipal works to make sure that only very clean water is returned to the sea. Reed beds of many types follow the aeration and flocculation tanks and and are themselves followed by several hectares of marsh and heavily wooded ponds. The wetlands became a picnic site and people camped there overnight. However, the wildlife, which also gathered, was so abundant that occasionally the bird droppings increased the phosphorus level in the final outlet (admittedly from practically nothing to slightly measurable), above the level entering the wetlands!

oxygenation by other plants, and sometimes producing toxins.

Sulphur Sulphur is ubiquitous in small quantities throughout organic matter. It is only very rarely a pollution risk, since its removal occurs automatically if the other determinands are removed. Therefore, in sewage treatment very little is attempted specifically for its removal or transformation. Any removal that occurs as all the other processes are underway is good news and gratefully accepted.

Because of its low water pollution potential, sulphur concentration is not usually monitored in sewage treatment.

The sulphur determinands are:

Sulphide — S_2^-

Sulphite — SO_3^{2-}

Sulphate — SO_4^{2-}

Hydrogen sulphide (H_2S) is the most obvious one to the nose of anyone in the region of anaerobic breakdown of the sulphur compounds — it is responsible for the well-known 'rotten eggs' odour.

With aerobic breakdown, the main product is sulphate, which remains dissolved in the water and becomes sulphuric acid. This can give concrete a lot of trouble, bringing manholes to a very interesting state; the walls become friable and crumbly, like a meringue coating. Special cement mixes are required for high sulphur contents. In anaerobic conditions, metals too can react, giving a black coating to valves and fittings.

Pathogens Leaving analysis of the chemical components of wastewater, we now turn to biological determinands. Sewage carries a multitude of potentially pathogenic organisms (see Introduction), the removal of which is essential if water-borne disease is not to be transmitted.

How do we find out whether water is potentially contaminated with sewage-derived pathogens? We could look for the pathogens themselves, but they are present only in extremely low numbers, amongst a host of non-pathogenic bacteria. And although one cell is enough to trigger a disease, one cell among billions is difficult to pick out. So instead, it is established practice to look for specimens of the billions of non-pathogenic (or at least not necessarily pathogenic) bacteria that are always present in human faeces. These bacteria are called indicator species.

The most common indicator species is *Escherichia coli*, members of this group being known as 'faecal coliforms'. Faecal coliform concentration (strictly speaking, population density) — measured in units of cfu/100ml, i.e. colony-forming units per 100 ml of water — is the determinand for bacterial contamination of water. Faecel coliforms are rod-shaped bacteria that have certain unique characteristics (to do with the way they eat sugar at 44ºC), so they are easily spotted. Furthermore, they live almost exclusively in shit. So if you find them in water you know shit has been in the water, fairly recently; that human pathogens may also be present now; and that you should avoid drinking it. The legal drinking water standard says that even if there is only one faecal coliform bacterium cell in a quarter of a pint of water (i.e. 1 cfu/100ml), you should not drink the water.

Of course, your sewage effluent will not be cleaned to the standard of drinking water and you will not be expected to achieve this. In fact in the UK a faecal coliform standard is (currently) not required to be met for effluent discharge to inland watercourses, because the risk to human health is considered to be minimal. Faecal bacteria are inevitably much reduced in number by the processes occurring alongside the removal of the BOD and SS. It is presumed that anyone who drinks water from a river downstream from a sewage outlet will sterilise it first and that people don't swim in rivers (well, only a few of us!).

So what are the pathogen-killing processes occurring in your sewage treatment system? In general, the longer a pathogen finds itself removed from a host organism, the more likely it is to perish. In liquid-sewage treatment systems processes fatal to pathogens include:

- being eaten by bigger organisms (especially protozoa);
- adverse physical conditions (such as too low a temperature, or too high a pH);
- the presence of anti-bacterial compounds (produced by some plants, as well as by other microbes);
- competition for food with other microorganisms.

A worked example

Now that we have looked at the main biochemical determinands, we are in a position to examine some real data and gather some meaning from the exercise. Fig. 4.6 (overleaf) shows a set of results taken from various stages of a real sewage treatment system (Fig. 4.7). By applying your newly acquired understanding you should be able to tell something about the way this particular system is functioning.

Line 1 The first line shows the concentrations of determinands of the liquid collected at point 1 on figure 4.7. These amounts are typical of primary effluent. The BOD is 250, which is average for septic tank outflow. As a rule of thumb, and we must prepare ourselves for many a rule of thumb here, almost half the total BOD of incoming sewage is retained in a standard septic tank. SS is a little bit low here since, as another rule of thumb, we would expect SS and BOD to be about equal in domestic sewage. The TOC can be taken on its face value as being 68 mg/l and used simply as another comparison for the progression of the carbon transformation.

Looking at the determinands of nitrogen, we see that the majority of the N is in the form of ammonia, indicating that no nitrification has yet taken place, and reinforcing the suspicion that this is septic tank effluent. Nitrite-N is very low as it almost always is, and TON is as low as the sensitivity of the test can measure. So we can say that there is almost no nitrate present.

The phosphate-P concentration is typical for a domestic situation.

—————————Reed bed monitoring—————————

	Susp Solids	BOD +ATU	Amm N	Nitrate N	Phosph P	TON	TOC
Septic Tank Effluent	134	250	38.0	0.082	13.0	<0.5	68
Primary Reed Bed Effluent	86	113	26.0	6.7	11.5	10.0	28.5
Feed to Iris Bed	50	53	21.5	2.55	12.0	9.0	16.0
Mixed Reed Bed Effluent	6	8.5	6.9	0.029	8.0	3.4	7.1
Final Effluent	2	4.0	11.0	0.104	9.0	3.4	8.2

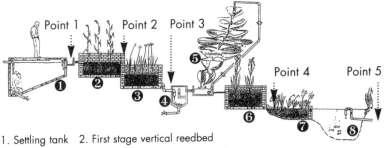

1. Settling tank   2. First stage vertical reedbed
3. Second stage vertical reedbed   4. Settling tank
5. Flowforms   6. Third stage vertical reedbed
7. Fourth stage horizontal reedbed   8. Pond

Figure 4.6. NRA analysis of a small (reed bed) sewage treatment system.
Figure 4.7. The sampling points of the small sewage treatment system monitored.

Line 2 What do the figures at sample point 2 tell us? From a simple scan of the figures we notice that concentrations have all fallen except for the nitrite and TON. If these figures related to your own system, at first glance you might have been a bit worried that you had something increasing in there, but on reflection you can take heart, as you realise that the rise has occurred because ammonia is beginning to be converted. Notice that, although a great deal more of the nitrogen is in an oxidised form, the total of 36 mg is very similar to the total of about 38 mg at sample point 1.

It is tempting to assume that there has been a quantitative transfer of N from ammonia to an oxidised form of nitrogen, by nitrification. Indeed, as a general indication this is a valid assumption. However, experience has shown that it is likely that, within stage 2 of the treatment system, further ammonia is likely to have been produced from the degradation of organic-N. Knowing this, the results suggest that some N has been lost as ammonia gas and some lost as nitrogen gas via denitrification. However, the figures provided do not inform us of whether this has happened and to what extent. TKN analysis would have helped us to make this assertion with confidence. The nitrite figure is unusually high — an anomaly we must live with.

The phosphate-P measurement indicates a slight reduction through stage 2.

Line 3 No need to dwell on the BOD, SS and N figures of this line. All the figures indicate that the processes we would like to occur continue.

However, somewhat surprisingly we see that orthophosphate-P has risen again. Possible conclusions:

- perhaps some polyphosphate has been degraded to orthophosphate;
- perhaps the test is within its sensitivity and statistically the 'changes' are insignificant;
- since the samples were taken within a few minutes of each other, the water which has arrived at the latter sampling point was predominantly from a washing machine, which used phosphates in the washing powder and the water higher up the system was from a sink, which has been released after washing down some vegetables.

We cannot readily distinguish between these possibilities from the figures provided. And that is another thing to get used to — dealing with probabilities.

Line 4 In the fourth line we see quite dramatic changes: everything is significantly reduced. Not only has *transformation* of the contaminants occurred, as witnessed by the BOD, SS, TOC and NH_4^+-N figures; but also their removal from the water stream, as indicated by the TON, and orthophosphate-P concentrations. We can conclude that both aerobic and anoxic zones have been encountered between the last two samples.

Line 5   The final water is of a high quality, far above usual legally required discharge standards. The trend of contaminant removal has continue up to sample point 5 but for one exception: the NH_4^+-N concentration has risen, and by an extent beyond the error margin of the tests. Perhaps further degradation of organic-N has occurred at this late stage in the treatment plant. Or perhaps sample 5 (which is not directly related to the foregoing samples since the water takes several days to pass through the system and all the samples were taken within 10 minutes of each other) was taken from a point that just happened to be carrying a relatively high level of ammonia produced some time previously and not yet removed. In fact, in this case, the latter is more likely since these samples were all taken at a natural treatment system which is in several consecutive stages ending in a pond. It is at this pond that the sample five was taken. Knowing the system it is possible that there was a reservoir of higher ammonia from the natural variation in treatment over the days.

Regulators and Regulations

Having become familiar with the sort of criteria that the authorities use to assess water quality, it is time to consider the authorities themselves.

Current Uncertainties

Much of the details of the following discussion are not cast in stone. This is because:

1. Several changes are occurring, regarding both the regulators and the regulations themselves. In England and Wales, the National Rivers Authority (NRA) has merged with Her Majesty's Inspectorate of Pollution (HMIP) to form the Environment Agency (EA). In Scotland, the River Purification Boards have merged with Her Majesty's Industrial Pollution Inspectorate to form the Scottish Environment Protection Agency (SEPA). Thus, two new environmental super-regulators have been created.

2. The current regulations are open to different interpretations; so different individual regulating people apply the regulations in different ways. Thus you can encounter (sometimes profound)

differences in different localities.

3. Related to the second point, many of the regulators are unclear about their designated roles, so they involve themselves in areas which, strictly speaking (according to Acts of Parliament) are not their concern.

The Regulators and their Roles
Town and Country Planning Department

The 'planning officers' of your local district council (or equivalent) may already be affectionately known to you by other less official terms, for unsympathetic decisions relating to some matter or other of local interest. Nevertheless, these people are your friends! Planners have a job to do and guidelines to follow. They are human beings and respond best in your interests if treated as you would like to be treated.

So what is their interest in your present plight? Well, they have a responsibility to ensure your plans for sewage treatment are in accord with other developments in your locality. For instance, it may be that other nearby houses are already exploiting the river at the bottom of your garden to capacity; in which case your desire to add to the exploitation will be frowned upon. In general, the Planning Department will base their ruling on the assessment of the environmental regulators (EA, SEPA, etc), whose opinion they will seek. Even assuming the environmental regulator is happy to let you discharge (at a certain effluent standard — see below), the planners are in a position to turn down your application for a treatment system if they deem it inappropriate.

Building Regulations Department

Building Regulations Officers (BROs) have a duty to ensure that the installation or erection of equipment or buildings conform to relevant parliamentary acts and/or British Standards. The British Standards guidelines are not statements of law, so if you do not conform to them you are not behaving illegally. But the BRO may judge that your work will not be or has not been done 'properly' and may thus refuse to grant permission for installation or indeed require you to remove or dismantle your construction. To which you might justifiably reply "Bother", so it is as well to take note of the BRO's advice, which you are at liberty to seek.

The Building Regulations are themselves constantly being reviewed and assessed. At the time of writing, the current regulations and standards, including BS6297:1983, are soon to be modified, in line with the many developments since 1983. Watch this space!

Environmental Health Department

Environmental Health Officers (EHOs) will not generally be asked to take an interest in your sewage system unless there is the possibility that a nuisance (e.g. foul odour) or health hazard may be created by the presence or absence of a treatment system. Usually the Planning Department will ask the Environmental Health Department to assess the situation if it seems necessary. This is most common when the system in question is unfamiliar (such as compost toilets).

EHOs have the power to make you take steps to meet their health, safety and nuisance concerns. They will not usually tell you what route you should take; it is up to you to submit a proposal that meets with their approval. That may mean obtaining clear evidence that your proposed system will work. Well established precedents are the most persuasive arguments in such cases, especially if the precedents exist within your district.

Environmental Regulators (EA, SEPA, DoE (NI))

These organisations have wide-ranging responsibilities regarding waterways. These include protecting rivers from pollution, so that human health and the health of the organisms that would normally inhabit the water are not adversely affected. The regulators have the right to prosecute you if you do not meet the effluent quality standards they have set for the particular circumstances.

The standards for many situations are becoming stricter all the time. This is worth bearing in mind if you want to avoid having to implement a costly upgrade in years to come.

The Regulations and Tariffs
This section covers:
1. Discharge Consents (the legal standards that your effluent must meet)
2. Discharge Costs (yes, it may cost you money to discharge your effluent)
3. Possible Scenarios (of your interactions with the authorities, when attempting to install your own treatment system).

Discharge Consents
When you approach the appropriate regulatory authorities (the local district council and/or the environmental regulators are your first ports of call) and tell them you want to discharge your sewage into a watercourse, they will insist that the sewage meets certain standards. The environmental regulators will send you a form to fill in, and will probably pay you a visit to assess your particular discharge situation. All being well, the environmental regulators will be happy for you to discharge and will then issue you with a statement of the quality that your effluent must meet. This statement is the 'Consent to Discharge'.

When it arrives in the mail, you find you have a "consent of 20:30". What does this mean? That one of your eyes must have vision like superman? That the ratio of pee to poo must be 20 to 30? Is 'Consent 20:30' a raunchy holiday package? Stranger questions have been asked and with careful reading of this chapter you can avoid such *faux pas* at the next sewage enthusiasts' ball.

The two figures, 20:30, refer to BOD and SS, respectively. They are the goalposts set for us by the authorities who have the overall picture of the health of the water environment in mind (see Box 4.8).

If you are given a discharge consent of 20:30, the regulatory authorities are telling you to make sure that there is no more than 20mg BOD and 30mg SS in every litre of sewage you discharge back into your stream.

Other forms of consents exist. You may receive a 'descriptive consent', which simply requires that no obvious pollution results from your discharge and that your system is maintained. There is also the situation where a system does not discharge to a water-

────────Box 4.8. Royal Commissions────────

Concern over water quality is not new. Early concern was expressed in Chadwick's 'Poor Laws' in 1850 and the Sewage Commission met in 1857. The most focussed panel of concerned scientists who met to consider a strategy to deal with water pollution was called The Royal Commission. These panels put out nine reports between 1898 and 1915 and set a standard for discharge of polluted water to rivers. They recommended a standard of 20mg/l BOD and 30mg/l SS — hence 20:30 — into watercourses having an average flow rate of at least eight times the flow of the discharge. This figure held for a long time as the standard and is still known as the Royal Commission Standard. Nowadays, many situations require stricter targets.

course. In such cases a consent to discharge is not necessary, although you are obliged to inform the environmental regulators of your discharge.

Discharge Costs

The EA calculates the cost of making a discharge based upon several factors:

1. The *annual fee*, which takes into account inflation and other costs. For reference, annual fees for recent years have been:

1991-92	£270
1992-93	£324
1993-94	£389
1994-95	£389
1995-96	£401
1996-97	£415

2. A factor for the *volume* being discharged, by which the fee is multiplied (discharge volume is calculated as being 90% of the water entering the premises each day):

0.3 for under 5 cubic metres of combined outfall. (If containing pure sewage, no charge, i.e. a factor of 0.)

0.5 for 5 to 20 cubic metres per day, even if just sewage.

If the volume of your discharge is greater than 20 m³/d, you would be well advised to bring in someone experienced in sewage treatment system design and installation.

3. A factor for the *pollution content* of the water being

discharged. Domestic sewage is given a factor of:
    3 if defined by numeric consents (BOD: SS etc.)
    2 if solely defined on its volume.
  4. A factor for the *type of receiving water*:
    0.5 if to soil
    0.8 if to the sea
    1.0 if to a stream or river
    1.5 if to an estuary.

Example 1 If, in 1996 (£401), a four-person house discharged the typical volume of 0.6-0.8 m^3 a day of nothing but sewage (factor of 0), with a consent of 20:30 (factor of 3), to a stream (factor of 1.0), then the householder would be liable to pay £401 x 0 x 3 x 1.0 = £0 for that year.

Example 2 If, in 1997 (£415), a 40-person community, consented on the basis of discharge volume (factor of 2), discharged 6-8 m^3 a day (factor of 0.5) to the soil (factor of 0.5), the community would have an annual charge of £415 x 2 x 0.5 x 0.5 = £207.50.

Possible Scenarios

To illustrate your potential relationship with various authorities, let us consider the following scenario. Although this is a somewhat extreme example (just to keep you on your toes), it is a description of events that happened in 1995-96. The basic principles apply, whatever treatment system you intend to install.

You have no existing sewage treatment system, and you have decided that a compost toilet (see page 113) is your preferred option. So, as recommended in the Designer's Flowchart, (see page 117) you set about to "check that authorities approve".

The first consideration is your proximity to the mains system. If you are within 30 metres or so of a sewer, the planners, possibly — but not necessarily — guided by the environmental regulators, can oblige you to connect to it. If you are further than 30 metres away, off-the-mains sewage treatment of some sort becomes a viable option in the minds of the authorities.

But compost toilets are often unfamiliar territory. So the planners pay you a visit to assess the lie of the land.

If there is plenty of land, they will usually expect you to explore the option of a septic tank and leachfield. This would involve conducting a porosity test, as specified by the environmental regulators (or in BS6297:1983), etc. It is in your interest to construct as efficient a leachfield as possible, lest you end up with a smelly bog in your garden, or pollution from your treatment system enters the nearest watercourse, at which point the environmental regulators will be in touch!

If there is an obvious watercourse to discharge to, and insufficient land of the appropriate porosity for a leachfield (the septic tank outlet must be more than 10 metres from the watercourse), the planners may well suggest a secondary treatment system.

However, you want a compost loo! It may well be up to you to familiarise the authorities. You are breaking new ground and most members of the council or environmental regulators will be totally unfamiliar with compost toilets.

So you argue your case for a compost loo, on ecological grounds. An EHO may well contact you, alerted by the planners. This is the person to convince. Present your precedents. Ask your local authority to contact other local authority departments that have granted permission for compost loos in the past. Compost toilets, being the most ecologically-minded sewage treatment available (although not always appropriate, nonetheless) can also be argued for on grounds of the local council attempting to meet its obligations re. Local Agenda 21. Ask your local council for details of its activities in this regard.

Finally, the EHOs and thus the planners are convinced. It makes so much sense, they are wondering why they didn't think of it before. So you get the blessing of the local authority? Maybe.

Summary

Assessment of the extent to which a sewage treatment system is achieving its aims is possible using a range of techniques. These vary from simple DIY tests to more complicated biological and biochemical laboratory methods used, for instance, by the regulatory authorities to assess and maintain standards.

Laboratory tests determine the concentrations of a number of 'determinands', the most frequently assessed being BOD and SS. By understanding the relevance of changes in concentrations of these, as well as other determinands, it is possible to assess the performance of a treatment system. Such understanding is useful for design.

Several regulatory authorities exist to offer advice, as well as to set and maintain standards pertaining to installation and modification of sewage treatment systems. Planners, Building Control, Environmental Health and environmental regulators refer to each other as appropriate, in assessing the most suitable way forward for on-site disposal on a situation-by-situation basis. The growing familiarity of the authorities with novel treatment methods allows a wider choice of approaches to on-site disposal.

Chapter Five
Avoiding the Generation of Blackwater

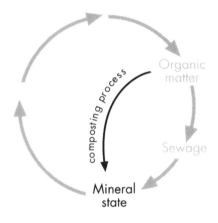

The Big Circle chapter described sewage as organic matter in water. This chapter considers whether it was such a good idea to add organic matter to water in the first place and whether it might conceivably have something better to do than hang around the sewers kicking up a stink. The chapter is divided as follows:

1. From muck into gold — the process of making humus
2. How to make humanure
3. Returning humanure to the soil.

From Muck into Gold — The Process of Forming Humus

Things have been dying and decaying for much longer than sewers have been around. What used to happen to things that were decaying before we flushed them away? Presumably they fell down wherever they happened to be at the time. This is true whether we're talking about someone relieving themselves a short distance from the settlement or about an animal that dies in the wild. The shit or carcass will fall onto soil. It will not be left alone for long; creatures will emerge as if from nowhere, gorge themselves, burrow in the organic residues and in the surrounding soil, gradually to turn the organic matter into more soil.

Soil versus Water

In chapter two we saw that oxygen is vital for the efficient breakdown of organic material. In a soil with high humus levels we might expect about 50% of the volume to be space occupied by water or air. In such soils there is lots of oxygen available since air is about 20% oxygen. This is not the case in a body of still water where not only is it rare to have 10 mg of dissolved oxygen per litre, but also what little oxygen is there travels 10,000 times slower than it does through air.

This brings us to the slightly shocking realisation that the problem with sewage is not so much that there is organic matter in the water, but that there is water around our shit. (Both are valid ways of looking at the situation.) Because the water prevents lots of oxygen from reaching the organic stuff, it stops a rapid and useful decomposition of our muck and leaves us with something that isn't particularly useful to man or beast.

So why do we use water? The reason is transportation — water helps move the sewage down the pipes and away from us so we don't have to deal with it right away. But by using water we create a problem: two valuable resources have been turned into one poison.

Humus

When organic matter is on the surface of a lively soil we can expect a fair amount of the material to be released to the air, particularly as carbon dioxide due to microbial respiration. Another fraction of the organic matter is eaten by larger organisms which find the waste to be to their liking. These will slither, waddle, and fly away to their own miraculous life cycles and will eventually contribute their own droppings and carcasses to the same process.

The part of the soil that is made of organic matter is called *humus*; and it's fascinating stuff. Humus has (at least) three important qualities:

- it contributes to soil structure
- it provides energy and a relatively stable form of nutrients
- it retains nutrients and water.

These qualities are worth a little more scrutiny. There is a continuum of states of humus defined by two fractions. One is the organic matter which sticks around in the soil for a long time and which can be called gross structural humus. (Lawrence Hills calls it 'soil furniture'.) When it was in an organism it was also part of its structural element. The other fraction is the colloidal (see Box 5.1) one formed either from rapidly decaying matter that once had its origin in the more vital parts of the organism or from the gradual attrition of the structural matter.

For example, structural humus such as lignin is produced from the heartwood of a tree, whilst the colloidal humus will be formed from such origins as young leaves, fruits, or the excretions of animals that have fed upon the various parts of the tree. Material high in BOD quickly provides energy and will become colloidal directly, whilst the material with less BOD will first become structural material and then slowly break down into colloidal material. As with sewage, the breakdown of these organic residues releases nutrients which plants may then take up.

Topsoil is made up of various states of this humus, along with the mineral elements of the soil, particularly clay. Worms will blend these elements together to form small clusters which stick together and give the soil a crumb-like structure full of air spaces. These spaces are also the passages through which water will travel as it makes its way through the soil.

Thus there is a gradation of stability of topsoil from the essentially immortal clay and mineral fraction: the long-lasting structural humus, the relatively short-lived colloidal humus, and the transient liquids (soil solution). Apart from the clay, these other humus fractions are able to change from long term nutrient stores to readily-available nutrient or soil solution.

The colloids are the front line — the zone of activity and interaction between plants, moisture, and nutrients. Generally the surfaces of these colloids are negatively charged, so they will bind

—————————————— Box 5.1. Colloids ——————————————

'Colloid' is a term referring to one phase of matter (solid, liquid, or gas) dispersed within another. This differs from one phase dissolved within another. For instance liquid dispersed within a gas is fog, and solid dispersed in a gas is smoke. Solid dissolved in liquid is a solution (sugar crystals in tea), contrasted with solid dispersed in liquid which is called a gel. It is this last type of colloid with which we are primarily concerned when talking of the colloidal nature of humus and the smaller mineral particles. In doing so we follow a rather loose but widely used meaning of the term 'colloid'.

positively charged ions such as potassium and magnesium. The positively charged ions can be exchanged for hydrogen ions from the plant roots, making the previously bound elements available for the plant. In this way too, humus acts as a reservoir of vital nutrients and minerals, preventing their escape in solution.

The other vital aspect of humus is its ability to hold water. A soil rich in humus is able to hold many times the quantity of water than the mineral elements of the soil can retain. However, this water is able to exist alongside the humus without a significant leaching of the nutrients. Thus plant roots have a choice whether to make use of clean water for transpiration or to absorb nutrients from the store of humus for their uptake.

This can be contrasted with discharging a mineral solution on to soil. In this situation the majority of the soluble elements (particularly the nitrate) will wash through the soil and have very little chance to add to the humus. Furthermore, plant roots in contact with the mineral solution are unable to avoid taking these salts into their tissues. There is evidence to suggest that because of this, the plants grown with an overabundance of these soluble nutrients are not as healthy as their soil-grown relatives. Hydroponic vegetables (i.e. those grown in an inert support matrix and provided with nutrients in solution) don't have the flavour of soil-grown plants, and their seed quality is not up to that of mother strains grown in soil. Hydroponic plants are also more vulnerable to disease, and they require special breeding to survive.

The Choice

Thus we have a choice between adding organic matter to water or leaving it to decay upon the soil or in a compost heap. If we add it to water, we are creating a poison whose water element is ruined for most uses and whose load of nutrients is either leached through any porous medium upon which it is placed, or taken into plant tissues at the expense of their overall health.

Alternatively, if we make humus of it, we are stopping the final breakdown of the organic matter at a minute 'colloidal' particle size rather than as a solution. The colloids will retain nutrients, improve the long term health of the top soil, and grow healthy plants. Furthermore, once this organic matter is stabilised in the soil as humus, that soil becomes much better at absorbing any later addition of nutrients. A humus-rich soil acts as a sponge for further decomposition or for nutrient application.

The Challenge of Making Humus

The transformation of shit into humus seems a consummation devoutly to be wished. However, such 'humification' can only occur in certain conditions. If, for instance, organic matter is decaying so quickly that anaerobic conditions arise, the picture changes. This can happen, for example, because the BOD of the decomposing material is not met by the oxygen available. The organic matter begins to form a black slime, like the stuff one can sometimes see around muck heaps; the rain has washed material down to the soil surface, which is itself compacted from the creation of the heap. Water accumulates from the rain and can't get away because the drainage is affected by the compaction of the soil, exacerbating the anaerobic conditions. This makes the organic matter into what is known as a gley. It is a mixture of organic matter (usually either sappy plant matter or dung, both of which have a high BOD), the organisms trying to flourish upon it, and a lot of moisture. Whilst gley production may be a useful process for someone who wishes to seal a pond, for productive soil it is just a problem.

To avoid formation of this gley requires some thought. A possible way around this is to spread the organic matter over a large area of land as is done when farm manure is spread over crop

——Compost Toilets——

Figure 5.1. The pedestal of a compost toilet. Some models have a screen over the hole which retracts when a person's weight is on it.

land. But when we are dealing with our bodily wastes we also have to consider whether chucking it around outside is going to have repercussions on our health and how we are going to manage the process. What is done in practice is to make use of less area, and make sure that structural organic matter and the more rapidly decaying organic matter of our excrement are combined in the right proportion. In the literature of such considerations this is referred to as getting the 'carbon-to-nitrogen ratio' correct. Carbon is dominant in structural organic tissue like wood and plant stems, whereas nitrogen tends to be found more in the sappy and vital centres of plants or in excrement. Combining C and N in the right ratio so as to form rich humus is most often achieved by creating a well-drained compost heap.

How to make humanure
Composting Toilets

The discussion so far has been a build-up by way of introducing you to the composting toilet. We have done this because if you are familiar with the concepts outlined above, you will be able to maintain a compost toilet in good working order. The second reason is to show that compost toilets are not new-fangled gadgets without the pedigree of a septic tank or other recognised sewage systems; they are a balance between the ancient methods of the countryside (abandoned as inappropriate when urbanisation became so prevalent at the time of the industrial revolution) and the hygiene requirements of modern society.

Box 5.2. Soak

Soak is usually a carbon-rich material such as sawdust, wood shavings, or straw. Other materials can also be used, such as wood-ash or lime, but although these have the effect of smothering the scent of recent contribution and absorbing some of the moisture, they do not add carbon to the nitrogen-rich pile and they do not provide an open structure. For these reasons, when attempting to achieve ideal composting conditions, carbonaceous soak materials are preferred. Paper and cardboard are also OK, although they are not so good at smothering the dung and preventing smells. There is some indication that mixing the carbonaceous soak with soil actually reduces nutrient loss, by clay particles binding gaseous ammonia. So it is likely that the ideal soak is a mixture of chopped straw, soil and a touch of mature compost to seed the pile with organisms.

What are compost toilets? Their purpose is to make human muck innocuous without using water to flush it away. At first glance, a compost toilet may look like a usual WC. But when you lift the lid of the pedestal, the usual small pool of water is absent and in its place is a chute — usually rather dark. You do what you came in to do and then, instead of flushing, you throw a handful of what is known as 'soak' (see Box 5.2) down the chute from the container you have put by the pedestal. Do not search in vain for the flush handle and throw a bucket of water down the chute in despair. Simply close the lid and leave the room with the knowledge that you have just made a small but significant step towards recycling your muck.

What is beneath the chute has a theme and variations. The theme is that there is a vented, drained chamber which receives the faeces, urine and soak. The vent, which may be assisted by a fan, extracts any odour generated from the pile. Usually the vent will also take air from the toilet room, thus removing the necessity for any other extractor fan. Apart from the drain, the chamber is closed in all other respects to exclude rodents and flies. The exit of the vent is usually covered by fly mesh to prevent the escape of any flies that do manage to find their way in.

The chamber is drained from the bottom to remove any excess (and surprisingly inoffensive) liquid. Access is provided for

The Clivus Multrum composting toilet

Figure 5.2.

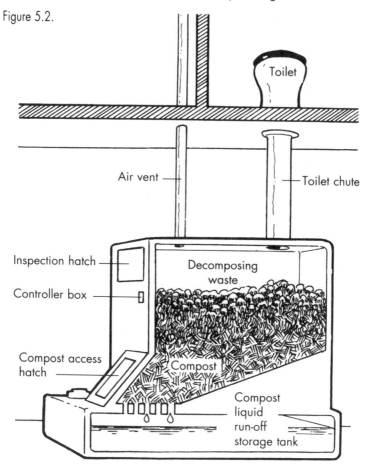

removing the accumulated humanure, no longer recognisable as what you know it to have been.

The variations upon this theme are many and you are referred to *Fertile Waste* and the Resource Guide for suppliers and manufacturers.

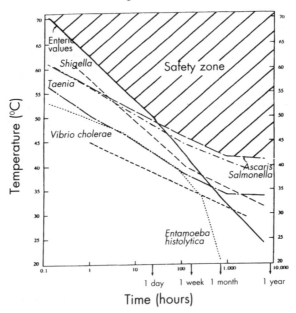

Figure 5.3. The effects of time and temperature on human pathogen mortality.

Compost toilets and health

There are many pathogen-killing processes that occur in composting human manure on its way to becoming soil. Time is a major factor (Fig. 5.3) since the majority of human pathogens die within a few months, if not sooner, once outside of the body. Exceptions include *Ascaris lumbricoides* and *Strongyloides stercoralis*, nematodes that can survive for several years outside the human body if conditions are optimal.

High temperature is another means of killing pathogenic organisms (Fig. 5.3). All human pathogens die if kept at 55°C for three days. So if you know your entire humanure pile has experienced these conditions you're OK. But this is very difficult to ensure. Since compost toilet piles rarely heat up (as a thermophilic compost heap in the garden would do), there is still concern about

——Box 5.3. Compost Toilets and Pathogen Death——

Clivus Multrum Inc, a company making compost toilets, has undertaken research into the material that leaves their toilets. Clivus has been awarded a seal under standard 41 of the National Sanitation Foundation scheme in the USA. Their work shows bacteria counts in their compost loos to be at least 10,000 times less than in sewage sludge from a septic tank, and a similar result was found for the liquid which drained from the installations when compared to septic tank effluent. Indeed, the faecal coliform count was found to be lower than the recommended maximum for swimming quality water by an average of ten times! Current evidence indicates that it is advisable to leave the pile as untouched as possible for two years in the UK climate, or for seven years if *Ascaris* worms are known to be carried by people in your area, which is very unlikely in the UK. After this time the pile is pathogen-free.

---

the efficacy of pathogen removal in compost loos. However, there is evidence to suggest that even mesophilic (well below 55ºC) composting — such as occurs in the Clivus Multrum (Fig. 5.2) — is just about as effective at killing pathogens as the hot composting process (see Box 5.3).

Researchers at the Liverpool School of Tropical Medicine are currently studying material from the twin-vault compost toilets (Fig. 5.4) at CAT to try to work out exactly how long faecal coliforms and known pathogens can survive in the piles.

Two of the great challenges of composting are maximum nutrient recovery and humification in the shortest possible time. Prolonged studies on humanure of both these aspects have been undertaken (see Box 5.4), with great success. Nevertheless, challenges remain, even in these respects, since the unwieldiness of relatively complete nutrient recycling may well seem somewhat off-putting to most, and obtaining a hot humanure pile remains an elusive art.

The challenges of composting human muck

Apart from the taboos (see below) and the health and safety aspects (both of which we acknowledge and consider very

The Twin-Vault composting toilet

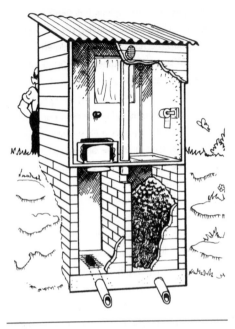

Figure 5.4.

One full vault is left to compost for a year while the other is filled up. The first is then emptied out and the seat swapped over.

important) concerning humanure, there are a few other potential problems with composting toilets.

Human turds can sometimes be surprisingly resistant to break-down, and excavated composting toilet containers some-times reveal something very recognisable even after several years of hibernation. Although we have not seen authoritative research, the collective wisdom of the authors considers that there are a few reasons for this. The first is that with all the minerals, particularly from our urine, there can be very high salt levels in the composting vessel. The delicate membranes of worms and other degrading organisms cannot manage such a salty environment, so these essential degraders do not thrive. The second is that the material is often too dry! Okay, we know we are the ones who suggested not putting water into the toilet but this is exactly what we are now suggesting you might consider. A little moisture in the composting vessel can really work wonders for the mesophilic organisms who would love nothing better than to turn the contents to a beautifully structured, inoffensive and useful humus.

A product known as the Domestic Organic Waste Management and Utilisation System (which is understandably better known by its acronym DOWMUS, Fig. 5.5) takes this very seriously. This is an

────Box 5.4. How much land do you need?────

A fascinating study of what might be achieved with excrement has been conducted by John Beeby of Ecology Action, USA. Using simple mass balance calculations and experimentation on that basis, he has made and collated meticulous research into the size amount and makeup of the materials required for maximum retention of the 'fertiliser value' of humanure.

Beeby aimed for maximum reclamation of the nutrients in humanure by ensuring that the ideal carbon to nitrogen ratio (i.e. about 30:1) for a mesophilic humification process was present in his composting piles. He discovered that, owing to the low C/N ratio in humanure (see below), the astonishing amount of 15 cubic metres of carbonaceous material is required in order to retain most of the nutrients of just one person's annual production of faeces and urine. He then went on to work out the minimum land area required in order to grow this amount of carbonaceous material, and which would receive the humus produced to grow the food that would sustain the person producing the humanure in the first place. Dedicated work!

Joseph C Jenkins an independent researcher, also in the USA (who coined the term 'humanure'), has achieved thermophilic composting process for humanure. The process loses more nutrients but has the benefit of quickly killing off the pathogens.

Both have published their work, Jenkins in his *Humanure Handbook* and Beeby in *Future Fertility* (see the Resource Guide).

Australian development and is, in some respects, counter-intuitive.

The details of the generic compost toilet design hold good for the DOWMUS, although the suggested soak is all the paper and cardboard from the house. In some cases the only water that is added is the water from the sink in the toilet room and this makes for a very good, cool composting process. However, with careful sizing all the rest of the water from the house can be passed through the composting heap as well.

This deals with another drawback of other composting toilets,

The DOWMUS composting chamber

Figure 5.5.

Greywater is added to the composting pile to facilitate the humus production.

which is that they do not treat the 'greywater' — all the other dirty water in the house such as showers, sinks, washing machines. It may seem strange that the solid waste from a house may be a great 'filter' medium for treating the greywater — it is not the obvious thing to do to pour relatively clean water over a growing heap of what might be called household crap. But this is what is done in the DOWMUS and the result is very encouraging. The organic material does exactly what it does in a moist top soil and becomes a structured humus, thriving with all sorts of microorganisms eating and being eaten, taking organic matter up and down and maintaining good drainage (Fig. 5.6). The wastewater which passes through this structure is also treated and emerges at a very acceptable level of cleanliness. All this is achieved on a household scale in a container approximately the size of a septic tank.

This also means that the DOWMUS can be used where the authorities will not allow non-flush toilets and there is no reason why this shouldn't take over the world. (We are enthusiastic about this one!) Work is underway both to make this process robust and

───────How much water?───────

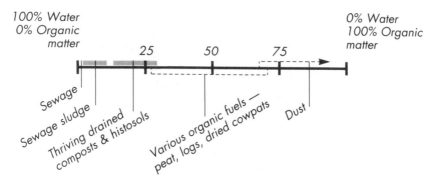

Figure 5.6. Graphic representation of the proportions of organic matter and water in various materials.

successful in this climate and to make it an accepted technology for the regulatory authorities.

A final drawback of composting toilets is that they require some space under the seat — and this usually means in the floor below. For many people this floor below does not exist or is too precious to fill with a box of ordure! Composting toilet designers have developed some clever designs which make use of moving parts to increase the space available (Figs. 5.7, 5.8) without going down into the cellar (see *Fertile Waste* for further details).

Urine Collection

Separate collection of urine offers the benefits of both saving water and recovery of nutrients, since roughly 73% of the nitrogen and 46% of the phosphorus we excrete is in our urine (see Box 5.5). Fresh urine is generally sterile, making it relatively safe to handle. Collected urine can be diluted with at least five parts water and used as a plant feed, or added to a carbon-rich material such as cardboard or straw to make compost.

The simplest way to collect it is to keep a container in the loo with a suitable funnel and lid (Fig. 5.9).

The Rota-Loo composting toilet

Figure 5.7.

The Naturum composting toilet

Figure 5.8.

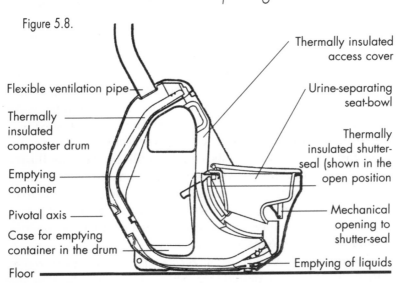

Flexible ventilation pipe

Thermally insulated composter drum

Emptying container

Pivotal axis

Case for emptying container in the drum

Floor

Thermally insulated access cover

Urine-separating seat-bowl

Thermally insulated shutter-seal (shown in the open position

Mechanical opening to shutter-seal

Emptying of liquids

——Box 5.5. What is in your faeces and urine——

	faeces	urine
Approx quantity:		
	135 - 270g/per day (moist weight)	1 - 1.3 litres per day
	35 - 70g/per day (dry weight)	50 - 70g/per day (dry solids)
Approx composition:		
Moisture	66 - 80%	93 - 96%
% dry basis:		
Organic matter	88 - 97%	65 - 85%
Nitrogen	5.0 - 7.0%	15 - 19%
Phosphorus (as P_2O_5)	3.0 - 5.4%	2.5 - 5%
Potassium (as K_2O)	1.0 - 2.5%	3 - 4.5%
Carbon	40 - 55%	1 - 17%
Calcium (as CaO)	4 - 5%	4.5 - 6%
C/N	5 - 10	0.05:1
Total dry basis:		
N	3g (6% of 50g)	8.5g (17% of 50g)
P	2g (4% of 50g)	2g (4% of 50g)

Source: Gotaas, Harold B. *Composting: Sanitary Disposal and Reclamation of Organic Wastes.* WHO. Monograph series No. 31, Geneva, WHO. 1956. pg 35.

A more refined way is to use the Ekologen urine-separating toilet (Fig. 5.10). This clever appliance has a built in 'funnel' in the front of the normal toilet bowl to collect urine. This is flushed with only 0.1 — 0.2 litres of water. The urine is collected in a remote tank for use on compost heaps or as a liquid fertiliser. The main flush is typically 5.0 — 7.0 litres and is adjustable. A non-flushing simple chute model is available for use on dry toilets. Since the toilet relies on the user sitting on it for urine collection, a sloping ceiling or wide shelf may be needed to prevent men standing to pee and could even keep the seat dry!

There is some research that suggests that urine can be stored for a long time if kept cool and away from faeces. Some bacteria that

Urine collection

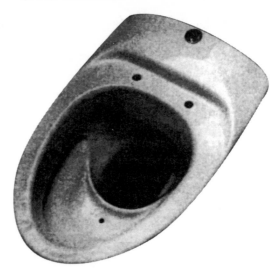

Figure 5.9 (left). Back to basics: a pee can with lidded funnel will do the trick for collecting urine to use as a fertiliser.

Figure 5.10. More advanced: an Ekologen urine-separating compost toilet model with seat removed for clarity.

---

degrade urea are found in faeces, and keeping them separate from the urine will prevent the urea breaking down to ammonia (provided it's kept cool) and thus from smelling.

Having now brought composting toilets into the scope of this book we can insert the Designer's Checklist of System Types and the Designer's Flowchart (Figs. 5.11 and 5.12 — see pages 114-117). (Although these might seem more appropriate to chapter three we have postponed them until this point so the comparison is simpler.)

Electric Toilets and Chemical Toilets

Whilst on the subject of avoiding making sewage by keeping the organic matter out of water, we should mention other toilets which don't have a flush.

Electric toilets (Fig. 5.13) are toilets in which the excrement is

The Mullbank electric toilet

Figure 5.13.a.

The Biolet electric toilet

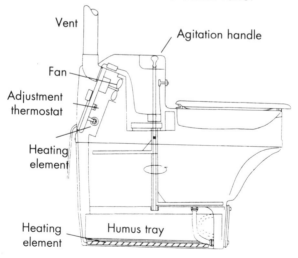

Vent

Agitation handle

Fan

Adjustment
thermostat

Heating
element

Heating   Humus tray
element

Figure 5.13.b. Cross-section of a Biolet electric toilet (courtesy of Wendage Pollution). Models exist using zero electricity or varying amounts, depending on the number of heating elements and the thermostat settings.

Figure 5.11. The designer's checklist of system types.

System	Land Use	Sludge Disposal	Effluent Quality	Wildlife Value
Performance range	Low ———— High	Low ———— High	Good ———— Poor	Good ———— Poor
Dry Toilets	May be difficult to retrofit	Dry compost low volume	None or very little	Forest floor ecology
Cesspool	Access needed	Expensive as no sludge separation	None on site	
Septic tank and leachfield	Land above field can still be used	Removal by tanker every one to five years	Very good	
Package plant	Buried	Usually yearly by tanker	Medium	
Vertical flow reed bed	Medium	Sludge drying bed often included	Good	Fair
Ponds	High	Infrequent but depends on design and climate	Medium to good	Very good
Horizontal flow reed bed	Medium to high	Settlement or septic tank, remove by tanker	Poor to medium unless tertiary stage, then very good	Good
Trickling filters	Low to medium	Settlement or septic tank	Medium to good	Fair

Energy Use excl. sludge disposal	Capital Costs	Running Costs	Odour and fly nuisance	Maintenance
Low High	Low High	Low High	Low High	Low High
Low unless heated	Low if self build, no pipes etc.	Very low unless heated design	Good with proper design	Basic and can involve shovelling
	Medium	Frequent emptying	Good	Emptying
	Medium	Low (sludge disposal)	Good unless leach field has failed	Preventative maintenance could save leachfield
Electricity	High	Electricity, sludge disposal and spares	Generally good	Service contract common
	High unless self build	Sludge disposal	Fair, occasional smell possible	Simple gardening and ongoing awareness
None to high depending on aeration	High unless self build but depends on site	Electricity and pump repairs if aerated	Fair to good	Gardening
	Medium	Low	Fair to good	Low
	Medium to high	Low but spares expensive	Fair	Medium

System	Ruggedness	Aesthetics	Notes
Performance range	Good Poor	Good Poor	
Dry Toilets	Depends on designs but needs awareness	Can be very beautiful or a smelly hole	Tackles the problem at source, possible regulation problems
Cesspool	100% reliable until full!	Underground	What a hassle, but don't be tempted to knock a hole in it
Septic tank and leachfield	Good	Underground	Least cost and impact. Effluent dispersal if site suitable
Package plant	Fair	Usually underground	Many designs, some very good. Need electricity. Benefit from horizontal reed bed after
Vertical flow reed bed	Good. When it fails, does so slowly	Messy to beautiful	Don't be seduced by the green package
Ponds	When it fails, does so slowly	Messy to beautiful	Robust and reliable but probably needs aeration in the UK climate
Horizontal flow reed bed	Good	Messy to beautiful	We only recommend them for tertiary treatment
Trickling filters	Fair	Looks like a sewage system	Work well, can benefit from a horizontal flow reed bed on the end

Figure 5.12. The designer's flowchart.

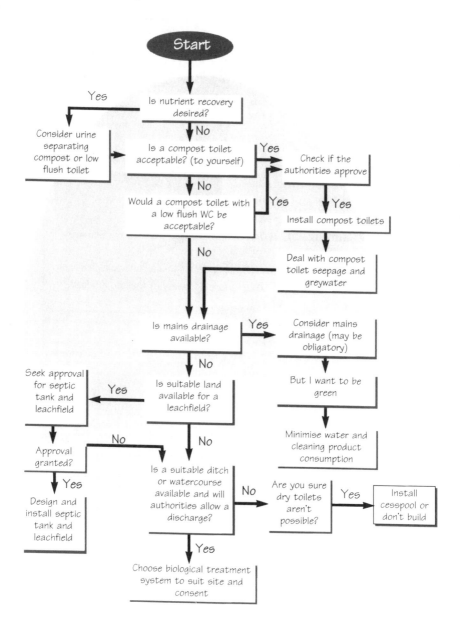

Chemical toilets

heated to dry the matter to an inoffensive powder which can be returned to the soil or put in the dustbin. They are often called compost toilets, but strictly speaking this is not true, as it is not 'composting' but cooking within the chamber.

These toilets can be successful in their aim of avoiding plumbing, the contamination of water, and further treatment, but since they are not really aiming to work within the Big Circle and because they use (sometimes quite large amounts of) electricity we will not dwell upon them further except to say that there are a few types

Figure 5.14. The Porta-potti chemical toilet (courtesy of Thetford Products).

available in this country. As with the brands mentioned above we refer you to the Resource Guide.

Another way is to store the matter in chemicals and then throw out the chemicals and the matter within. These chemical loos (Fig. 5.14) have been used in, for instance, caravans and building sites for many years but their limitations are clear. They are there to avoid connection to the mains and to keep the toilet matter from smelling and attracting flies. But it is really just a holding exercise and does nothing to work within the Big Circle.

Returning Humanure to the Soil
A Word of Caution

The time will come to empty your composting chamber and do something useful with its contents. You may be surprised to find that, even with all the soak you added, the total volume is no more than a wheelbarrow of humanure per person per year.

You will naturally take all the appropriate precautions when handling the compost, even though it may be no more full of pathogens than normal soil.

So where should you put it? The best use of its potential is to work it into the topsoil with a hoe around the plants of your choice. It may be best to avoid leafy vegetables or herbs.

As there are no government guidelines for humanure reuse some officials have classified it together with sewage sludge, which does have restrictions concerning its application to the land. In fact this restriction is irrelevant as the material is quite different; for one thing it does not contain metals, caused by the common practice of combining industrial with domestic sewage.

If you are unsure as to the quality of your humanure then you might like to plant a tree in it, after digging a suitable hole. Ensure that drinking water is not abstracted nearby and avoid high water tables, so pathogens have no chance of entering a water supply.

Whilst we are confident about our methods of recycling humanure and the significance of doing so, there is a certain caution with which we would like to infect our readers.

There are many cultures that have a taboos regarding human muck. It is not just a prudish Victorian problem reflecting a general uptightness and discomfort with anything to do with the body. The reluctance to touch humanure or to use it on food plants is shared by Muslim, Jewish, Maori, and some African cultures, and surely they are not all easily classified as stuffy. At best, human muck is regarded as useless stuff, and at worst as something negative. This in itself would make a fascinating study, but it also raises the question of whether there is something we might learn from such attitudes to human muck.

Perhaps these taboos are from the historic periods of such cultures when they did not conceive of disease as having water-borne organisms at their root. Thus the taboo may have reflected empirical wisdom and was perhaps just another way of saying, "It can make you sick if you deal with this stuff, so don't bother". However, for several reasons we would like to suggest that the "Should I or should I not use humanure?" debate isn't left there because that might not be all there is to it.

First, if we suggest that you draw your own conclusions as to how safe humanure is, it 'covers our backsides'. It really is a personal decision as to how you deal with humanure, from the

————————Box 5.6. The Maori and Water————————

UK settlers have a history of making a pretty thorough job of exterminating indigenous people and claiming the beach and all concessions for the monarch. However, the Maori of Aotearoa (New Zealand) have survived the colonial process better than most, enough for their cultural perception to be fairly well represented on planning boards.

In Gisborne, on the far east coast of the land of the long white cloud, the council is already gearing up for the great sunrise — Gisborne will be just about the first place on Earth to see the sun rise in the new millennium, and it is hoping to attract a great many people for the event.

However, the sewage systems of the town are already overburdened, and sewage is poured out to sea. This is not the way of the Maori. *Waimaori* (water touched by humans) is considered *waikino* (corrupted). But, as with all water, it is still sacred and must not be put into pipes and be disposed to sea; it must go to the land. What will happen?

---

extent to which you ensure hygiene in the toilet, to whether you apply mature humanure to your food crops.

Second, several companies building sewage systems in the UK (and the author of this section runs one of them) are influenced in one way or another by a school of thought called anthroposophy. And the prime mover behind anthroposophy, Dr Rudolf Steiner (1861-1925), was good enough to offer his opinion upon the results of using 'nightsoil' on human food crops. "Nothing could be worse," he said; and he was not talking about possible stomach upsets. He meant that food grown on human waste made it less able to support that part of each of us which has the potential to raise us above the level of animals.

This is perhaps thin ice and the source of great debate between the authors whose opinion ranges from "bizarre rubbish", to "strange, but worth trying to understand Steiner's reasoning". Perhaps we shouldn't easily dismiss this; he has been proven right in many ways since saying such things at the turn of the century, especially in matters of digestion; it was he who expressed very specifically and accurately what would happen if ruminants were fed animal protein. Steiner also showed his method of working, thus distinguishing his opinions from *ex cathedra* statements of other enigmatic folk.

Anthroposophy (also known as supersensible science) does not limit itself to evidence of what can be measured or weighed. It offers itself as no less scientific than a 'material' science and thus is accessible to scientific scrutiny. The debate will continue amongst the authors, who would welcome thoughtful comment from anyone who might throw further light upon this.

However, the main reason (upon which we all agree) for dwelling on this is to reinforce a real sense of caution, essential simply in pure hygiene terms. It may be frustratingly slow to turn around the cultural momentum (currently in favour of water-borne sanitation) but there are real dangers in poorly handled muck. Sloppy work with compost toilets is bound to harm any potential progress towards their wider adoption as surely as stubborn officials. Any method of dealing with human waste should be undertaken carefully and any product which is for sale must be of a high standard. The nightmare of the authors is that the eloquent persuasiveness of this book initiates a rash of stinking heaps of shit attended on all sides by flies and sick children.

In the hope of intercultural dialogue, and recognising our common physiology, we leave this chapter with an anonymous irreverence from the Internet...

Taoism	Shit happens
Confucianism	Confucius say, "Shit happens"
Buddhism	If shit happens it really isn't shit
Zen	What is the sound of shit happening?
Hinduism	This shit happened before
Islam	If shit happens, it is the will of Allah
Quakerism	Shit happens to everyone
Catholicism	If shit happens, you deserve it
Presbyterianism	We never talk about things like that
Judaism	Why does shit always happen to us?
Agnosticism	What shit?
Atheism	I don't believe this shit

Summary

Possibly the most environmentally benign method of on-site disposal is to convert toilet waste into humus, thus avoiding the use of water for transport and minimising sewage generation. Other resources minimised include pipework (to and from the toilet) and treatment facilities. The humus generated is a stable, organic material with many features beneficial to soil and plants.

Humanure (humus generated from composted human faeces and urine) can be hygienically produced using a modern compost toilet. Many designs exist, some allowing separate collection of urine (which carries the bulk of the plant nutrients found in our bodily wastes) and others achieving simultaneous treatment of household waste and greywater.

Mature humanure may be safely applied to the soil. It should be borne in mind, however, that certain cultural taboos exist in this regard which are usually not without foundation. Personal consideration may be required in order to reach your own conclusions.

Chapter Six
Using Domestic Water Wisely

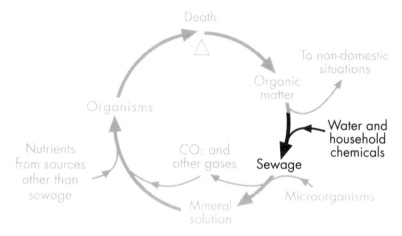

When it comes to making a sewage treatment system work, nothing is more effective than controlling what goes down the drain. The preceding chapter offered one approach to those who can install dry toilets. The remaining water in the home can also be used wisely. That is the concern of this chapter, which is arranged in two main sections:

1. What you can put down the drain.
2. Water conservation in the home.

What you can put down the drain

You have built your sewage system and don't want to kill it by pouring harmful chemicals down the sink. Or perhaps you have an existing treatment plant that is under-performing; or a leachfield that is getting a bit wet and smelly at times and you wonder if the problem is what you are putting down the drain.

Well, by definition that must be the problem, since if you don't put anything down the drain your troubles will be over! Whilst this may seem a trivial observation, a reduction of your discharge volume can be a very cost-effective approach, particularly in situations where there is nowhere suitable for treated wastes to go or where space for treatment and disposal is limited. First let us look at the chemicals carried in your greywater, under two broad headings:

1. Detergents and household cleaning agents
2. Other chemicals.

Detergents and Household Cleaning Agents

Two common questions asked by people with their own sewage treatment system are, "What detergent should I use?" and "Is it OK to use bleach to clean the toilet?". The answer to both questions, to the best of our knowledge, is that all of the systems discussed are robust enough to handle normal amounts of household detergents and cleaners. A soggy leachfield will not be cured by a change of detergent brand. If your effluent is consistently poor and you suspect a particular substance is causing the problem then try a couple of weeks without putting these chemicals down the drain and see if there is an improvement. If you know of reliable research on this subject please let us know.

Having said there is no problem, if you are concerned about the wider ecological impact of your actions, you will want to use the most ecologically benign cleaners you can find and in the smallest effective dose. We would have liked to offer a top ten rating by greenness but there are no clear answers. One problem is that many different factors have to be compared and we are left with the sort of sums that we were told as kids were impossible, such as what is two bananas minus one apple, as we try to equate transport energy with biodegradability with pollution at the factory. Nevertheless, we can offer you some pointers (Box 6.1).

One example of this is the 'zeolite versus phosphate' debate. Phosphate is added to most washing powders as a 'builder', to regulate pH and improve the action of other ingredients, as well as preventing dirt from resettling on the clothes. Phosphate in our waterways is responsible for eutrophication (see chapter four) and the formation of algal blooms. Since around half the phosphate in sewage is from washing powders it would seem sensible to use phosphate-free powders.

———————Box 6.1. Cleaning agent elements———————

1. Biodegradability: by law, all detergents are now at least 80% 'biodegradable' according to a recognised standard (OECD test), but some are more biodegradable than others.
2. Bleaches: washing powders, toilet cleaners and dishwasher powders usually contain chlorine-based bleach. The chlorine can combine with organic compounds to form highly toxic, and carcinogenic, organo-chlorine compounds. Non-chlorine bleaches are available, and washing powders with separate bleach are a good choice (for several reasons).
3. Phosphates: phosphates are added to washing powders (but not to washing-up liquid) to soften the water. They can lead to eutrophication in watercourses.
4. Optical brighteners: these substances do nothing for cleanliness but give an illusion of whiteness. Problems include allergic reactions, poor biodegradability and mutation and inhibition of bacteria in your treatment system.
5. Other additives: NTA, EDTA, enzymes, preservatives, colourings, synthetic fragrances, etc. are all suspect in terms of ecological impact in production and final disposal.
6. Zeolite: possibly a more benign replacement for phosphate. It is an inert mineral, but it can can encourage algae problems in sea water and comes all the way from Australia.
7. Sodium: common salt (sodium chloride) is used as a thickener in washing-up liquid; and soaps and detergents contain sodium ions, which break down the structure of clay soils and so reduce their permeability. Can be a problem for leachfields and greywater irrigation.
8. Manufacture, packaging, transport: however ecologically sound the final product, it is of little benefit to the environment if the manufacturing process causes significant pollution.
9. Political: it is impossible to look at ecological impact without considering the wider issues of fair trade, employee conditions, and a company's aims and ethos. Many of these issues are open to personal opinion so we leave them to your own research.

The usual alternative to phosphate is an aluminium-based naturally-occurring, mined material called zeolite A, which has to be used with a 'co-builder' called polycarboxylic acid (PCA), which

Great balls of zeolite

Figure 6.1. Eco-3 zeolite balls and Bion discs. Zeolites in the wash are considered by manufacturers to remove calcium from the water and replace it with sodium, making the water 'softer' and thus increasing the effectiveness of any detergent or soap employed. The manufacturers of 'Bion Discs' consider that no washing powder need be added to the wash and that they will remove dirt electrostatically. The manufacturers of 'Eco-3' give hints on removing resistant stains from the washing before putting in about 10% of the normal detergent load and their three dodecahedral balls.

---

deals with the dirt resettlement problem.

A report by Bryn Jones (ex-Greenpeace) sponsored by Albright and Wilson (who manufacture phosphate-based detergents) gave the phosphate-based builder an impact score of 107 penalty points and the zeolite builder a score of 110. Whilst this difference is quite insignificant, Jones claims that 30 to 40 points could be knocked off the phosphate score by introducing phosphate removal and recycling at sewage works. To add to the debate, Italian researchers have found zeolite to be implicated in the formation of 'sea scums' of algae.

If any of this is close to the truth, the main conclusion is that it is the quantity of washing powder that we use that matters, rather than the brand. A little of the worst will be better than a lot of the best. With detergents, enough is enough and more won't make the wash whiter. Some technical fixes are possible such as washing-up liquid dispensers to reduce indiscriminate squirting and balls containing a small quantity of zeolite (see Fig. 6.1) to put in the washing machine to reduce detergent use by up to 100%.

Our own experience shows that these products are effective for about 300 washes but the absence of perfumes and artificial whiteners (usually found in commercial detergents) can be noticed after a while. Anticipating this is as a problem, the manufacturers of Eco-3 supply essential oils to add to the rinse water.

Considered from the point of view of sewage treatment these approaches are particularly likely to have an impact in situations where detergents are used in great quantities (laundries, nursing homes) and where the water is hard. In the latter situation the soaps combine with the calcium to form 'soap lime', which can clog the matrix of percolating filters or other fixed film process treatment systems.

So, a lot depends on individual situations. If you irrigate your garden with your wastewater then use phosphate based detergents in summer and grow big plants! If your sewage system discharges into a particularly sensitive body of water such as a Scottish or Irish loch then use phosphate-free detergents and let your sewage system remove the zeolite (ideally discharge to land).

If all the apparent confusion has taken the wind out of your sails please don't be discouraged and please keep your ear to the ground for news of more ecological cleaning products, as there is clearly room for improvement, both in the products and the new discipline of environmental impact assessment (EIA). Clearly some detergents are more biodegradable than others and contain less harmful additives, such as brighteners or artificial scents. It is just that we are at present unable to offer a firm recommendation with full confidence.

If the choice between pollution of the sea bed off Morocco (from phosphate mining) versus open cast Australian bauxite mines (for zeolite manufacture) doesn't sit easily with you then all we can recommend is using as little as possible. There are books (see the Resource Guide) listing household alternatives to commercial cleaning products. We have become accustomed to thinking that we need a cleaning product for every household task, when often all we need is water, which is totally benign — when used sparingly of course!

Other chemicals

Sheer convenience can cause even the most conscientious of us to tip the occasional jar of white spirit down the drain when washing brushes. Once again small quantities should not kill your whole sewage system but they are likely to have some inhibitory effect on its organisms. The main concern is that such chemicals may receive little treatment and so end up in the stream or water-course where they will do harm.

One litre of white spirit could bring 100 million litres of drinking water above the recommended limit for drinking water! (The EC standard is 10 µg/litre for dissolved or emulsified hydro-carbons.) This is the volume consumed by half a million people a day. If you use such things as white spirit or photographic chemicals then it makes sense to collect them for responsible disposal or recycling, provided of course you can find somewhere to take them. *Ring the EA low toll helpline on 0645 333111 for details.*

Whilst, in an ideal world, we would all have a range of suitable containers for collecting these chemicals (or wouldn't use such chemicals), we recognise that very few people will take half a jar of brush cleaner to the Council's hazardous waste site. In this case, for occasional disposal of very small amounts of less noxious chemicals, the better of the possible evils is to sprinkle the offending liquid over a pile of soil or old compost. In the case of a liquid such as white spirits take the waste, leave it to settle, decant any clear liquid which may be reused, then allow the remaining liquid to evaporate and any residue can then be disposed on a suitable site in the garden or in the dustbin. But do not use on the vegetable garden in case the solvent contains lead or other residues, and do not do this if near a well or other drinking water supply. Please note we do not recommend tipping chemicals in the garden but it is one step better than down the drain. Meanwhile, we hope that attitudes and infrastructure will change to make proper disposal the norm.

——Box 6.2. *Household Solvents Disposal*——

Solvent	Disposal method
White spirit	settle, decant and reuse, dispose of solid in bin
Brush washing water	pour on dry soil (small quantities only)
Engine/gear oil	ring oil bank helpline 0800 66 33 66 for local collection point for recycling
Old paint and garden chemicals	ring the Environment Agency helpline 0645 333 111 for your nearest recycling point
Cooking oil	compost, recycling centre for larger quantities
Unused medicines	take to the chemists
Rainwater	divert to rainwater soakaway or butt for irrigation

For general advice also phone the Environment Agency helpline 0645 333 111.

Water conservation in the home
Why conserve water?

As we have seen, one of the most troublesome chemicals that we pour down the drain in copious quantities is water! Excess water can have a far greater impact on sewage treatment performance than the worst detergents and can lead to blocked or overloaded septic tank leachfields. Perhaps counter to intuition, strong sewage is easier to treat than the equivalent organic load in a larger volume of water. Added to this biological factor, increased flows can lead to reduced settlement in septic and settlement tanks and so more solids are discharged to overload the next treatment stage.

The most serious problem is rainwater (from roofs and paved areas), which must not be put into the sewage system. If we imagine 25mm of rain (an inch) falling on a 100m² roof we get 2,500 litres of water. This is the equivalent of about fourteen people's daily water use concentrated in the space of perhaps an hour.

You can check whether your rainwater drains are connected to your sewage system by using buckets of water and, if necessary, food colouring or drain tracing dye. Any offending drains must be directed to a separate soak pit in accordance with Building Regulations. Another potential problem is where old drains have cracked and so let surface water into the sewage system. This can be best checked immediately after rain.

Returning to water conservation. Once again there are wider ecological and financial reasons to save water, and the interested reader is directed to our sister publication *Safe to Drink* (see Resource Guide).

Reasons to save water
- To reduce the volume of sewage to be treated
- To reduce leachfield problems in heavy soil
- To survive drought without standpipes or parched gardens
- As a least-cost solution to meeting a growing need for water-related services, without flooding valleys or moving water by tanker or giant pipelines
- To reduce demand on precious groundwater supplies
- To reduce the threat to rivers caused by over-abstraction
- To reduce the energy used to purify and pump it
- To reduce the production and consumption of chemicals used to treat it
- To reduce the energy used to heat hot water
- To reduce water and sewerage bills
- To create meaningful employment developing, manufacturing, selling and installing water-saving technologies
- As a challenge
- As a hobby that doesn't need to satisfy strict payback periods to be valid

Order of priorities: Reduce, Reuse, Recycle
A general principle: it is almost always cheaper, more ecologically sound and less hassle to save a resource than to recycle it or to harvest and transport more of it.

For example, a low energy light bulb costing say £10 will save more electricity per year than the £400 wind generator powering this computer will generate in the same period.

Water use is no exception to this principle — it makes sense to apply conservation measures first. If we then decide to go the whole way and install rainwater harvesting, greywater recycling or the fore-mentioned wind generator then the capital and running costs of these systems will have been reduced and their effectiveness increased.

Unfortunately there is little glamour in turning off the tap while brushing your teeth or replacing the tap's washer when it drips. What we eco-philes want is a reed bed or rainwater system with pumps, pipes and valves to play with. The sequence below shows our recommended order of priorities for domestic water conservation, based on the above principle of reduce-reuse-recycle. Ok, it is not quite as neat as that, but you'll get the idea. We say this because it is not uncommon for the ecologically enthusiastic to go straight to number 6!

1. Develop awareness of use, and change to water-saving habits
2. Plug leaks, dripping taps and cisterns
3. Change or modify appliances
4. Reuse water, without further treatment
5. Harvest rainwater
6. Recycle greywater.

Let us look at each of these in sequence, in a bit more detail.

Developing Awareness, Changing Habits

The Domestic Water Audit Since water consumption depends on personal habits and variations in household plumbing, the first step to water conservation is to assess how much water is currently used and for what purposes. Keep a note of how often washing machines and other appliances are used and estimate toilet flushes and shower use. Measurements with a stopwatch and jug will help estimate water wasted whilst taps run hot or teeth are brushed. This is ideal work to get kids involved with. If a water meter is fitted you can check if the estimates add up to the measured consumption. This audit will identify the areas where most saving can be made and may show up some surprises.

Changing Habits Because most water is used in the bathroom and toilet, the biggest savings can be achieved by changes of personal habit, most of which are common sense. You may wish to take radical steps, such as pissing in the garden and not washing (not changing your habit, if you happen to be a monk). However, technical fixes are possible for those of you who want to keep your existing circle of friends.

Leak plugging

Although rather unglamorous, prompt replacement of tap washers, worn ball-cocks and flush diaphragms (the floppy polyethylene disk that acts as a piston to start the flush in a toilet) will save much wastage. A crude experiment with a jug and stopwatch suggests that even a slight drip from tap or ballcock can waste 30-40 litres/day (about 6 toilet flushes) and a steady dribble can easily waste water equivalent to having eight extra people living in the house — an enormous energy loss if it is a hot tap, and a real problem for many sewage systems and leachfields. If the flush diaphragm is worn or split, the flush will be inefficient, leading to multiple flushing and wastage. If you are not familiar with simple plumbing repairs but are willing to have a go, a good home DIY manual should give clear guidance.

A clever device (Fig. 6.2 overleaf) is now available that eliminates the need for an external overflow pipe from toilet cisterns (saving installation labour and heat loss from the room). At the same time, it makes the flush inoperative if the ball valve is leaking, forcing you to repair it promptly.

Technical Solutions — Changing and Modifying Appliances

Some of these result in improved functionality — such as aerating taps that don't splash, WCs with an efficient and quiet flush, basins plumbed so that they run hot almost instantly, and foot-operated valves to allow mucky hands to be washed without messing up the taps or risking contact with other people's germs. Here we shall discuss the following:

1. Toilets
2. Showers, baths and basins
3. Dead legs
4. Taps

The Seeflow overfloat

Figure 6.2.

5. White goods
6. Water meters
7. Gardens.

Toilets Flush toilets account for around 30-50% of household water use, so the potential for savings is large. Obviously dry toilets (chapter five) give the greatest saving (you saw that coming) but if you're committed to having a water closet, low-flush toilets are available and existing units can be improved.

The UK situation — the siphon flush   The UK is about the only place in the world (we are assured) still to use the siphon flush in the cistern. The earliest flushing mechanism was a valve which, being made of leather or rubber, was prone to leakage. The siphon flush (Fig. 6.3) was a great step forward — once air breaks the siphon no water can flow until it is started again.

The first problem with this clever improvement is that it offers considerable resistance to the flow of water. This means by the time the flush has got going, it is time for it to stop, resulting in low efficiency. Putting the cistern up high was a good way round this problem, but is now out of fashion.

The second problem is that when the floppy diaphragm that acts as a plunger to start the flush splits, replacing it can be tricky

The Siphon flush

Figure 6.3.

Removing the plastic plug allows air to enter and break siphon for half flush. Holding the flush lever down blocks the hole allowing full flush.

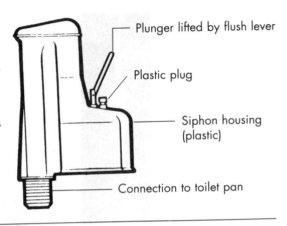

- Plunger lifted by flush lever
- Plastic plug
- Siphon housing (plastic)
- Connection to toilet pan

and is beyond the limits of confidence of many householders. Hence many houses have a poorly functioning toilet requiring multiple flushing.

As far as flush volume is concerned Water Byelaws now demand a maximum of 7.5 litres. Unfortunately this is often insufficient, given the poor design of many pans and flush mechanisms.

It is mildly amusing to consider that we are perhaps the only people in the world to share the familiar experience of a toilet that refuses to flush properly!

The rest of the world — the valve flush   The original valve-based mechanism is used almost everywhere except the UK and has come of age with the advent of modern seal technology (Fig. 6.4). The argument goes that even if the valve does eventually leak (ten years' life is claimed as typical) and is allowed to drip even for two weeks, the water saved in those ten years is far more than would be wasted in the two weeks. Added to this, seal replacement can be carried out easily without special tools, unlike the fore-mentioned flush diaphragms.

As well as giving a far more effective flush with less water, the valve system usually lets you interrupt the flush to give an even smaller flush for wee. This level of control, however, has what is referred to as a 'user interface problem' i.e. many people don't know how to use it. This has been tackled in Australia where the standard modern cisterns have separate, clearly labelled buttons

——The non-UK valve flush——

Figure 6.4. This 'Servo-Set' model is used to adjust the flush cycle and flush volume to cut water consumption.

for a three and six litre flush. In practice this gives an average flush volume of only 3.8 litres. By the time this book is in print a three and six litre dual-flush toilet will be available in the UK from Villeroy and Boch (see the Resource Guide).

European toilets are available in the UK but there is a possibility that you could have trouble with Building Regulations in new buildings due to the absence of a siphon, which is required by the Water Byelaws. Meanwhile, connection of a non-approved toilet to mains water supplies could result in a fine of £400. If you have your own water supply and sewage treatment then these Byelaws do not apply. The Byelaws run out at the end of 1996, to be replaced by something that could allow what is normal in the rest of the world; however, new regulations could take two years to come into force.

In Sweden, of course, they go a stage further. The Ifö Cera toilet (Fig. 6.5) achieves an efficient flush with only 3.7 litres of water (see Resource Guide). The Ifö is adjustable between three and eight litres and is set at the factory for six litres. The Ifö is now also manufactured with a dual flush option, as described above, and is supplied set for two and four litres.

We should also mention, as it has to be mentioned somewhere, the amazing waterless urinal, which can be installed in public and private toilet facilities anywhere, and which relies on its success to anti-bacterial herbal solutions, administered to the surface. The urine can be collected and treated or used as a nitrogen-rich fertiliser. Details can be found in the Resource Guide. The design is about 100 years old and well-tested; they are in use at the Centre

——— *The Ifö Cera toilet* ———

Figure 6.5.

for Alternative Technology. Easy to install, they could be used anywhere.

Making do with what you have Low flush toilets are a fairly expensive option if you already have a satisfactory loo, but there is a lot that can be done to improve on the standard model.

The simplest way to reduce flush volume is to bend or adjust the ball-cock, but this should not be done because it lowers the water level in the cistern and gives a poorer flush. It is better to use plastic bottles filled with water, arranged carefully so as not to obstruct the ball-cock and, if the overflow allows, to actually raise the water level by adjusting the ball-cock. The tricky bit is to calculate how small a flush you can get away with — too low a volume will lead to multiple flushing and thus actually increase your water use.

The old-fashioned practice of placing the cistern up high can provide a better flush than some low level slimline models and allows a larger reduction in flush volume without loss of efficiency. However, the bowl must be designed for this if splashing is to be avoided. Because the non-UK flush valve has a larger pipe and reduced restriction, it provides a vigorous flush with a low-level cistern.

Whilst savings can be made by fine-tuning the flush volume, further savings can be achieved by the use of a smaller flush for pee, which is what we do most in toilets. Many flush units (the plastic assembly inside the cistern) have the option of being used in the dual flush mode, usually by removing a small plastic plug (Fig. 6.3). If yours does not have this, then changing an old unit for a new one is a cheap and simple operation. With the plug removed, the lever is pulled and released for a half flush or held down for a full flush. Since the instruction sticker provided is rather unappealing it usually ends up in the bin, so visitors unfamiliar with such technology will probably waste gallons of water sussing it. This fact has led to dual flush siphonic units being outlawed by the Water Byelaws because they waste water! Despite their dubious legality they are, at the time of writing, widely available from hardware shops and builders' merchants. A suitable poem in framed calligraphy could provide the required information and serve as a reminder without offending the aesthetic senses. (A free copy of this book will be given for best suggestion sent in). Dual or interruptible flush toilets are common in the rest of Europe where, we assume, their function is understood.

Other technical fixes on the toilet One clever idea is the combined toilet cistern and sink, where the wastewater from hand washing is used for flushing. These have been used in Japan for decades but we have yet to see one in the UK. A commercial model is available from the US (see Resource Guide for the *Real Goods Living Source Book*), but a DIY model could be made. The obvious problem is matching hand washing to flushing. One solution might be an oversize cistern and a non-siphonic European flush valve to allow less than a whole cistern to be used. An overflow into the toilet bowl or to the original waste pipe would be needed and there could be problems with fermenting soap and hair (so flush the loo before going on holiday).

Showers, baths and basins Although showers are generally considered to use far less water than baths, consumer preference has pushed manufacturers to increase pressures and flow rates so that a modern power shower can, at a flow of 10–20 l/minute, use as much water as a bath (depending, of course, on how long you spend under there). Low-flow shower heads with smaller holes save water while maintaining the invigorating pressure, but they are not readily available in the UK at present and work best when used at mains pressure. However, there are restrictors available that are easily fitted and will at least limit the maximum flow rate.

Many UK showers with electric heaters are, by necessity, low-flow, since the seven to eight kW elements are only able to heat around 2.5 l/min to a reasonable temperature. 'Low-flow' is a

Box 6.3. Dead Leg Volumes

Corresponding to Pipe Bore

Pipe bore (mm)	Bore volume per metre (ml)
6	18
8	33
10	56
15	133
22	340

[1000 ml = 1 litre.]

relative term that seems to cover the range 1.5 to 10 litres per minute, so check actual flow rates and likely performance before parting with your money.

At the bottom of the flow range are showers using air compressors with a water consumption of around 1.5 litres per minute or less. Unfortunately, the American company making them has gone out of business.

Dead legs This is the length of pipe that the hot water has to travel through before it reaches the tap. It is reckoned that letting taps run until water emerges hot wastes 38,000 litres a year in the average American household. The standard solution, found in hotels and some larger houses, is to use a thermosiphon or pump to circulate hot water and so eliminate dead legs, but this incurs a very high heat loss. Complex systems with pumps, timers and temperature sensors exist in the US to alleviate the problem but a simpler approach is possible for buildings without excessively long pipe runs.

When installing sinks and hand basins, consider using microbore pipe (8 or 10mm copper) for the hot feed as it will run warm quicker (see Box 6.3). Flow rate will be reduced, giving further savings, but check with a knowledgeable plumber or the pipe manufacturer before installing a long run to ensure the flow will be enough. In fact, where the flow rate to a small basin is to be reduced for water-saving reasons, this is best done by using the restriction offered by microbore, otherwise reduced flow rate will lead to a long wait until the water runs hot.

————————The infra-red hand sensor tap————————

Figure 6.7.

An infra-red sensor above the outlet switches on the tap only when a hand is present. (Courtesy Pegler Ltd.)

New building and major refurbishment offers the chance to optimise pipe sizes and lengths to minimise dead legs. The use of a mains pressure hot water system allows smaller pipes for a given flow rate. Luckily baths, which require a high flow rate, don't suffer in quite the same way from dead legs, as some cold water is usually needed.

Taps: *hands-free tap* A nice technical fix for the enthusiast or gadget fan is a hands-free tap. Commercial taps with optical hand sensors (Fig. 6.7) are available but are rather expensive at present (see Resource Guide). A simple switch-operated model is quite easy for a competent electrician to rig up. In the DIY model a foot switch activates a solenoid valve enabling hands off operation, thus reducing the temptation to leave the tap running while you brush your teeth or scrub your hands. You can use the small amount of movement in most under-sink cupboard doors with ball-catches to operate a microswitch which switches on or off when you lean against the door (Fig. 6.8).

A double switch and an extra solenoid with suitable restrictor would allow a dual flow rate for hand washing and kettle filling. Using a low-voltage solenoid reduces any potential shock risk but introduces a small but constant transformer load unless the switch is placed on the mains side. While separate hot and cold valves are possible, mixer taps present a slight problem for direct conversion. A thermostatic mixer valve at the hot water cylinder provides a good solution and prevents waste and scalding while fiddling to

The DIY hands-free tap switch

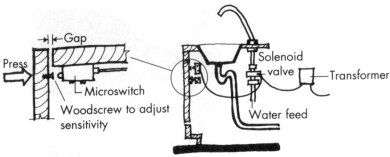

Figure 6.8. Plan detail of door switch. The operator's knee pressing against a cupboard door beneath the sink can switch on the tap.

get a bearable temperature.

Low-flow taps and aerators A simple trick for hand basins is partially closing the isolating valve that should be fitted on all recent plumbing fixtures, by law, to allow simple washer replacement without turning off the whole house water supply or draining down the hot water system. This reduces the flow rate specifically to the selected taps, saving waste as we rarely put the plug in when washing our hands or brushing our teeth.

Spray taps and aerators are designed to maximise the wetting capacity of a smaller flow and give the illusion of more water than is actually running. Add-on aerators are available in countries where mains pressure plumbing is the norm and taps are threaded to accept them. In the UK, taps incorporating aerators are available for use on mains pressure systems but will give a higher flow rate than typical UK taps, which often use a low pressure feed. There is no technical reason that we are aware of for not producing high-pressure low-flow aerators that could offer very low-flows for hand washing or dish rinsing. Perhaps the biggest selling point of aerators at present is that they reduce splashing at equivalent flow rates, a common problem with mains pressure systems.

Clearly, low-flow taps on a bath would be counter-productive. Bath size and shape determine how much water you need to get a given depth, and insulation will help keep the water hot, saving on top-ups.

The spray tap

Figure 6.9.

This spray tap is activated by hand pressure on the top and will remain on for an adjustable period of 10 to 30 seconds. (Courtesy Pegler Ltd.)

White goods With the introduction of eco-labelling it is now easier to find out and compare the water and electricity consumption of new appliances such as washing machines. Machines that use only 20 litres per wash cycle (compared with the normal 80-100 litres) are on the horizon. You can determine the water consumption of an existing appliance by discharging into buckets of a known volume.

Water meters There is little doubt that we are more careful when using anything that we pay for in proportion to the quantity we use. Water meters should allow the ecologically minded a small return on their investment in water conservation but the potential savings depend on installation costs, standing charges and other tariff structures. Some see water meters as a tax on cleanliness. Flats in some European countries have readily visible water meters in the bathroom which offer a constant reminder of water use as the numbers whizz round, indicating every tenth of a litre consumed. *Safe to Drink* looks at water meters, 'WaterKeys', and the economics and politics in more detail (see Resource Guide).

Gardens can consume gallons of water at a time of year when it is in shortest supply. Water-saving gardening techniques range from simple mulching (but beware of slugs) to growing drought-resistant plants, to relandscaping with clay linings under lawns. This is a complex subject as it involves living plants. For example, underwatering can be worse than no watering. See *The Natural Garden Book* and *Safe to Drink* for more details (see Resource Guide).

————Box 6.4. Reusing greywater————

— Sources in order of preference for ease of reuse

1. Shower and bath
2. Hand basins
3. Washing machine
4. Kitchen sink or dishwasher

Reusing water

Reuse involves using dirty water from one domestic activity for another, less critical, one without cleaning or treating the water in between. This is practicable only for greywater (see Box 6.4 overleaf) since blackwater would require treatment before reuse. We have already mentioned using hand-wash water for toilet flushing. The most obvious and commonly-practiced reuse of bath and other washing water is for the garden in hot dry summers. Some caution is needed, however, as sodium salts from soap and detergents can build up in the soil and destroy its structure, particularly in clay. Gypsum can be added to the soil to help neutralise this effect and details can be found in the Tipsheet *Reusing Greywater* from CAT (see Resource Guide). If greywater is stored without treatment it will quickly go rancid and smell incredibly bad — even we won't touch it.

Rainwater harvesting

Harvesting the relatively clean water that falls on our roofs is a very old technology, but the integration of rainwater into modern house plumbing is still at the experimental stage in the UK.

The importance and relevance of rainwater harvesting depends on the situation (see Box 6.5) and ranges from essential (Australian bush or remote allotment) to low priority (water supply from mountain stream in a wet part of Scotland). In the UK most households are connected to mains water, so we are faced with the question of whether it makes ecological or economic sense for such houses to have a rainwater system of some sort beyond a garden butt. The main choice is between a supplement to mains water and a fully autonomous water supply; the main difference is the size of

——————Box 6.5. Rainwater Harvesting——————

Pros and cons for domestic water supply

- Can be cheaper than a borehole or mains connection in remote areas.
- Gives the user control over the type of treatment and the chemical content of the water (e.g. chlorine, fluoride, aluminium are added to mains water).
- Reduces storm water flows, which overload urban sewage plants.
- Allows saving for and prioritising of water use, in drought.
- Provides a source of soft water for washing.
- Eliminates water bills.
- Requires minimal pumping energy, since collection is at the point of use.
- DIY system possible at low cost.

BUT —

- Puts responsibility with the users, so safety depends on their competence.
- Possibly high capital and maintenance cost.
- Possible problems convincing Building Control and Environmental Health Departments of safety.
- Requires either radical water conservation or large roof area and storage tank if no mains water is to be used during dry periods.

the cistern and level of treatment required. It has been shown theoretically that a storage tank of only 1,200 litres and a collection roof area of 50m² in Nottingham could supply 90% of the WC flushing water for a two person household. Increasing the tank size to 2000 litres was shown to give only a 3% improvement. If the water is to be used for toilet flushing, no treatment is required. Since reused polyethylene orange juice barrels with a volume of 1,500 litres are available for a reasonable cost, an economical DIY rainwater toilet flush system is feasible if space allows. However, don't expect an impressive payback at current water prices. Figure 6.10 overleaf shows the sort of arrangements required.

Be careful that your rainwater system complies with the Water Byelaws — the main concern is that mains water could become contaminated with rainwater through back siphonage. Having said that, we should point out that it is a myth that stored rainwater must go stagnant and breeds germs. Provided sunlight and organic matter such as leaves and dead animals are kept out,

Rainwater supply

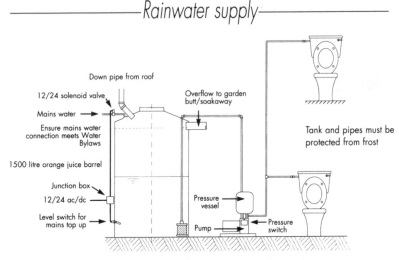

Figure 6.10. Plumbing arrangement for rainwater supply to toilets.

stored rainwater remains fresh and safe. As we have seen (chapter five) most human pathogens die (or at least cannot multiply) once outside the body. The organism that is of most concern is *Cryptosporidium*, a parasite transmitted in bird droppings.

Autonomous rainwater system   An autonomous system supplies all the water needs of the house from the rain falling on the roof. While this is the norm in the Australian bush and many other countries, there are few examples in the UK.

If spring or groundwater is available then this is almost always preferable to rainwater for consumption because of its purity and mineral content. You may want to collect rainwater for washing if the spring water is hard.

Where a borehole would be too costly or the water is contaminated, a rainwater system is a real possibility. At the time of writing the most recent example in the UK is Brenda and Robert Vale's autonomous house at Southwell, Nottinghamshire. The Vales have used the previously-mentioned orange juice barrels to provide 30m^3 (30,000 litres) storage, which has proved to be rather more than required.

Unless the collection area (usually the roof) is very large compared with the number of occupants, water consumption will have to be far lower than that of a normal household. The

————————*Rainwater supply*————————

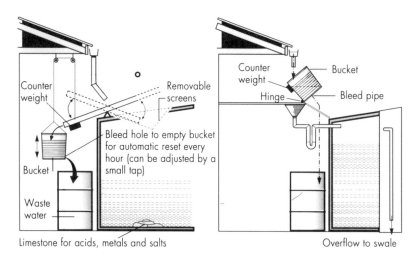

Figure 6.11. A device for rejecting the first flush of rainwater.

Southwell house incorporates a dry toilet and low-flow shower and is occupied by its designers, who are very careful not to waste water. Their daily water consumption is reported to be in the region of 140 litres/day for a family of four, compared with a typical family of four consumption in the UK of 480-800 litres/day.

Raw rainwater can be of good quality, but it is likely to be contaminated by small quantities of vehicle and industrial pollutants as well as pathogens from birds and mammals, so it needs to be treated to make it drinkable. Various technologies are available, including microfiltration, carbon or resin adsorption, UV radiation and chemical dosing. Generally, a combination is required, e.g. mechanical filtration followed by a UV unit, with an under-sink activated carbon filter for drinking and cooking water only. Consult a water treatment specialist before designing a rainwater system, and have the rainwater fully analysed before drinking it. Very soft water is implicated in heart disease and will dissolve metal plumbing systems, so bags of limestone chips (or other suitable mineral source) should be placed in water tanks to buffer the pH (unless the roof is concrete, which is alkaline). The minerals

The Wisy filter

Figure 6.12. Fitted to the downpipe from
can be used to reduce the amount of orga
in rainwater entering the storage tank,
thus preventing bad tastes and odours.
(Courtesy of The Green Shop).

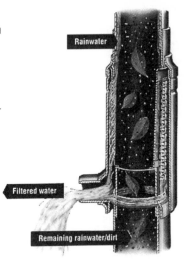

will also help precipitate out any
heavy metals that may be
present.

Several books refer to
ingenious contraptions to reject
the first (dirty) water off a roof
(Fig. 6.11) but such gadgets are
probably an unnecessary compli-
cation. The Wisy® filter (Fig. 6.12) is a simple self-cleaning device
for rainwater collection and initial screening.

This section has been intended to outline the possibilities of
autonomous rainwater systems, but full design of such a system is
outside the scope of this book. Further details concerning
harvesting rainwater, and the Vales' system in particular, are
provided in *Safe to Drink*. It is hoped that as more systems are
installed in the UK, a standard design will emerge.

Water recycling

It is possible to recycle household water many times, but this
requires energy and involves potential health risks if the water is to
be used for anything other than toilet flushing. Whilst treatment
systems can transform sewage into crystal clear, odourless water
with reasonable reliability, they cannot remove many of the
mineral salts and every single pathogen that is present and will
have trouble removing ammonia in winter. Moreover, even a small
amount of BOD will lead to stored water going anaerobic and
smelly.

While full recycling is technically possible (and essential in a
space station), we would argue that in the UK, if water conser-

either in terms of the volume of water we take from it or the quality of the water we return to it.

A correctly designed sewage treatment system (or even a simple septic tank and leachfield) discharging to the ground could be seen as a water recycling system replenishing groundwater.

If you are still determined to recycle wastewater for return to the house (e.g. for toilet flushing), start with the least polluted water from baths and hand basins, rather than the water from toilets or the kitchen sink and only use it for toilet flushing or, possibly, the washing machine (see box 6.4).

Reasons for recycling wastewater:

- To reduce the volume of wastewater discharged, e.g. where a house is served by a cesspool
- To water the garden in a drought (if the wastewater is untreated this is considered reuse)
- To irrigate as a form of treatment and disposal
- To supply a need for large quantities of low grade water, e.g. toilet flushing
- To use the heat from wastewater to warm a greenhouse
- To reduce sewerage bills (if you're metered).

Summary

Appropriate use of your water supply and suitable disposal of greywater are major aspects of on-site disposal. The chemical constituents of domestic greywater are unlikely to damage a sewage treatment system. In fact, discharge of excess water is likely to do mroe harm to treatment by reducing retention in the system.

Water conservation can have a major implications for successful sewage treatment and environmental impact. In order to minimise resource consumption, water-saving measures should be prioritised: reduce water consumption; reuse untreated, discharged water; recycle treated wastewater — in that order.

A range of technical suggestions and many appliances are available to help achieve water conservation.

Chapter Seven
Back to Life

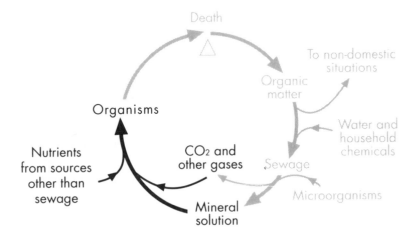

From discovering the ins and outs of sewage and its treatment and monitoring, we stepped back to explore how we can minimise our impact on the natural water environment, at the same time simplifying our task of refining our domestic discharge to the wider world. The final cleansing of our water — our mineral solution — we leave to the microorganisms, plants and animals of the natural environment.

This chapter considers the reincorporation of treated sewage into plants and animals of our choice, within the boundaries of our own land. It is organised as follows:

1. Humus
2. The Nutrient Solution
    Discharge to water
    Discharge to soil
    Aquaculture
    Irrigating willows
    Irrigating other plants
3. Life and the Big Circle.

Humus

Before we focus on introducing our *liquid* effluent to selected organisms' environment, let us indulge in one last cheer for humus, the final product of the composting toilet, when it is the material we have to reintegrate into nature.

Humus...

• is a stable form of nutrients
• is available to plants but not forced upon plants
• assists the soil structure
• increases the ability of soils to hold water in dry times
• increases the ability of soils to survive inundation in wet times
• stays put
• can exist with clean soil water without leaching of nutrients.

With that out of the way, and in acknowledgement that most people will have a liquid rather than humanure after treating their waste, we can look again at what might be done with the nutrient solution from sewage systems.

The Nutrient Solution

By one means or another, the sewage has been treated and flows to the end of your sewage treatment system. What remains is relatively clean water. As we have mentioned (chapter two), if your sewage has been treated to a secondary level there will be much that was originally in the sewage still present, but it is now transformed into a mineral solution. If your system includes some tertiary treatment, some of the minerals from the solution have been removed. (If your system includes a pond or some plants, some of the water may have evaporated or been transpired.)

In bringing the effluent as close as possible to a mineral solution — thus having transformed the organic matter well beyond the state of continual decay — we have done a great deal to solve the problem of sewage. Can we now do something positive with the liquid that remains?

──────────*Box 7.1. Blue-Green Algae*──────────

In the late summer of 1989 blooms of blue-green algae occurred in the UK, which killed some sheep and dogs and made ill a few soldiers who had been canoeing on the affected freshwater lake. The NRA quickly investigated the situation and put together a report. It concluded that some blue-greens exude poisons, but it is not clear what factors determine why a bloom forms or why it releases poison. Conditions that produce a bloom in one lake do not always produce a bloom in another and it is no surprise that the report recommends further research and monitoring.

While other algae thrive in the spring when the majority of nutrients are available, blue green algae have the ability to store phosphorus and thus outlive other species, blooming in late summer. Fertiliser runoff seems to be a relevant factor, but algal blooms have occurred long before the invention of artificial fertilisers. Warnings about algal blooms are part of the culture of ancient peoples.

It is worth noting that in 1989, when blue-greens caused such a stir, 135 people drowned in reservoirs and canals, but none died from blue-green algae poisoning.

Discharge to water

If a situation allows no positive use for it, then the effluent simply has to be thrown away. In most situations the only possibility will be to discharge the liquid back to the nearest part of the global water cycle, to a stream, river or coastline. If done directly, (i.e. without a leachfield) this must be done via a discrete pipe at the end of which the authorities can place a sampling vessel. This is a simple matter — you make the arrangement with the EA when you apply to make the discharge in the first place (see chapter four), and, when you build the system, be sure to leave reasonable access for the pollution control officer.

Discharge to soil

In some situations, a flow of water with a loading of minerals is exactly what is wanted. Plants need nutrients and water to grow, and they need to take up that nutrient in solution. Sewage effluent can provide this through hydroponic methods or direct irrigation to soil based plants. At the same time, the soil and plants will help to treat the sewage by mechanisms which include:

- oxidation of remaining BOD by soil microorganisms*
- nitrification of remaining ammonia*
- denitrification of nitrates
- bio-accumulation/absorption of all substances into biota*
- precipitation and filtering of suspended solids and metals*
- adsorption of minerals, particularly phosphorus to iron and aluminium
- predation and ultraviolet destruction of pathogens*
- cation exchange of metals*

Mechanisms marked [*] are appreciably better accomplished by a humus-rich topsoil than by the lower levels or subsoils.

Of these mechanisms, perhaps the most important is the removal of phosphorus through adsorption to iron and aluminium, especially in clayey soils. Too much phosphorus can cause algal blooms in receiving waters (Box 7.1). However, the removal of phosphorus is not simple and is rarely achieved with any consistency by sewage systems. Generally, any phosphorus removal that does occur is a 'good thing'.

Ideally, treated sewage should be discharged to the surface of the soil. Odour is unlikely to be noticeable; once domestic sewage has been relieved of its organic load, only a very slight stale, sweet smell of treated sewage remains. It is important, however, to check with the authorities that discharge to soil surface is possible in your particular situation.

Aquaculture

Another possibility is to practise aquaculture, which means growing animals and plants in water, usually for food (although you might like to cast a glance at the section on taboo (chapter five) before embarking on this discipline using sewage. (Hydroponics describes the method of growing plants in mineral/chemical solutions and aquaculture describes the gross set-up, so in practice they can, and do, overlap.) This is a very old use for nutrient-rich water and you can find more details in specialised texts (see Resource Guide).

An excellent charity named Plants for a Future publishes a leaflet on edible bog and pond plants cryptically called *The Edible Pond and Bog Garden* (see Resource Guide for details).

However, you can establish a very crude version of aquaculture to polish your effluent by encouraging algal blooms to occur to your advantage. In a sunlit pond filled with the sewage effluent, algae will occasionally flourish. Sometimes these will be surface algae that appear as a green tint or thin film. These will often be followed later by a billiard table finish on the surface of the pond (as when duck weed, e.g. *Lemna* spp, gets established). At other times, the whole body of the water turns various hues of green like pea soup. Sometimes the single-celled algae are joined by filamentous varieties, such as the blanket weeds, which seem to fill the pond with fibres.

This may not seem particularly advantageous, but the feverish eyes of a sewage cleaner see it as an opportunity. If one now discharges this algae-rich water on to soil, only excellent water will leave the property. First of all, algae bloom in spring and summer when the BOD of the water is relatively low. This means the ammoniacal nitrogen will be almost completely nitrified. Secondly, the soil receives the water with the minerals bundled into organic packets (the cells of the algae or *Lemna* plants) which can be filtered out much more readily by the soil than the same material when it is dissolved in water. These algae then decay on the soil surface where they can be incorporated into the soil as humus or, at worst, act as a slow-release soluble fertiliser.

This is now the basis for a type of treatment system and the Lemna Corporation, in the USA, has a wonderful machine for harvesting such plants from purpose-built lagoons (Fig. 7.1) receiving treated municipal sewage effluent.

However, if you're not going to discharge the algae-rich water to the soil or some kind of filter, you have to be careful. If the discharge of the water is directly from the pond to a watercourse, the pollution control officer will need to take a sample of water and put it through the tests for water quality. These tests are not sufficiently subtle to distinguish between various forms of organic matter, so they cannot tell the difference between the organic matter that was in the sewage before treatment, and something

Lemna harvesting

Figure 7.1. Lemna harvesting on a grand scale (courtesy Lemna Corporation).

relatively benign, such as algae, which has grown in the breakdown products of that original matter. So, you could receive an effluent analysis showing disappointingly high levels of SS and BOD, despite all your care.

Some countries, which are more familiar with pond sewage systems, make a 'chlorophyll allowance', recognising that, in a way, it is not fair to judge water full of algae in the same way that one would judge a sample with a turd in it. However, this is not the case in the UK, so you would be reprimanded whatever the nature of the organic matter in the pollution control officer's jar.

Irrigating willows

In practice, discharge to soil with or without intervening ponds, has been done in areas planted with willow.

There are two main strategies for irrigating the willows (although there are surely many more), which are readily adopted by DIY boffins. One is to divide the total area earmarked for

——————————*A willow plantation*——————————

Figure 7.2. A well-grown willow plantation irrigated with treated sewage using the trench method (Site System, CAT).

receiving the water into two or three smaller areas. Ideally, these areas are relatively flat and receive the water in succession. Every month or so a new section is put 'on line' and the previously saturated section is rested for two months. By alternating between saturation and rest, binding of the soil, which would restrict the permeation of the liquid, is avoided.

The second method of distribution is to make a channel, which meanders through the planted area (Fig. 7.2), allowing the water to ooze away through the banks of the channels and into the soil. The channel should fall at about 1:300 or so and is more appropriate for sloping sites. Again this can be done in rotation for the reasons mentioned.

Which plants you use will depend on what you want to do with them afterwards and on which ones will survive in the moist conditions they will meet.

If you are going to grow a stand of willows for chipping and burning, you'll need to provide access for harvesting machines. The faster growing willows would be chosen, so you might choose a variety of so-called 'super willow'. These are hybrids chosen for their vigorous growth.

Basket makers might prefer some of the traditional varieties such as *Salix triandra*, *S. purpurea* and *S.viminalis*. If you're growing the willow as a crop for craftwork, it usually needs to be clean and good quality, so you'll have to make decisions about herbicides and fungicides.

The young trees, grown from cuttings about 20 cm long, need a chance to get established without much competition for the first two years. We have done this with plastic mulches of left-over pond liner dug into the ground, with the cuttings stuck through them (Fig. 3.11.a). Others use bark mulches which seem to work fine. Otherwise, you'll need to return and weed the soil around the trees to make sure they get off to good start.

Irrigating other plants

If you want to make a wildlife habitat, use a variety of species. We planted one plantation with willow, poplar, and alder species, since they are known to tolerate saturated soils for part of their growing season. Oaks were planted into the bunds which divided the main planting areas, following a hint in the autobiography of Lawrence Hills, *Fighting Like the Flowers*. (The 'broken cycle' of fertility is something that also troubled him.) Oak is unbeatable at encouraging a wide variety of insect life and, therefore, increases the biodiversity of the whole area. (Willows are second only to oaks in terms of the number of insect species they can support.) Hills reported that the oak and walnut timber was of a high quality, even though the growth was greatly enhanced by being irrigated with sewage. One would expect that the 'forced growth' caused by the extra nutrient boost would produce a weak and sappy wood, but this seems not to have been the case. We added ash (the tree, that is), a heavy feeder, along with anything else we could get our hands on, in the name of diversity (and 'Agenda 21'). A fitting tribute to Lawrence Hills would be to use comfrey, bearing in mind his usual caveat of using a variety which will not spread.

Another possible plant would be *Formium tenax* or the New Zealand flax. This is a plant that looks like a bushy cactus, which the Maori use both for its strong and long fibres and for its

—————— *Box 7.2. Seidel and antiseptic plants*——————

One of the driving forces behind the recent development of reed beds came from the pioneering work of Käthe Seidel. One of her insights was that significant quantities of pathogenic bacteria died after passing through a horizontal reed bed planted with *Iris pseudacorus,* the familiar yellow flag. It was Seidel's opinion that the roots of yellow flag exuded an anti-microbial substance, and there is much to suggest that this is the case.

antiseptic properties. Perhaps its antimicrobial properties are due to the fact that it lives in wet marshy soils — perfect conditions for rotting unless a plant is able to protect itself.

One species that will no doubt volunteer even if it isn't planted (and will appear even if the water is treated to a very high degree beforehand) is the common nettle, *Urtica dioica.* Nettles are famous for their sting and also for gathering around muck heaps and septic tanks. They seem to favour soil rich with nutrients, and bring the soil to a beautiful tilth around their roots. If they are happy there then they are probably appropriate, although we haven't read any research suggesting what their specific sewage-treating benefits might be.

There are so many beautiful and useful plants that like plenty of nutrients and thrive in moist ground that the reader is referred to more specialised literature.

Life and the Big Circle

What really goes on when either decaying organic matter or mineral matter is incorporated into living creatures is a mystery not yet fathomed, even by modern science with all its incredible accomplishments. Whole cultures can be defined by the answer each gives to the question of "What is life?".

Although we will not attempt to provide an answer, we can offer a slightly less ambitious question for consideration — is life inherent in the matter which makes up the organisms or does something else get involved when matter is in tissues? Is life dormant in mineral matter and only an 'epiphenomenon' of the way it is arranged when within organisms?

These would be idle questions for long winter evenings if there

were not the possibility of an answer, and if there were not implications in practical life. The topic relevant here is 'Flowforms'.

Flowforms

Flowforms (Fig. 7.3 overleaf) are sculpted vessels, usually, but
not necessarily, of reconstituted stone, over which flows a constant
stream of water. There is one path or axis which gravity will
encourage the water to take but, due to the moulded contours of
the vessels, water is also encouraged to swing rhythmically away
from the axis into the depressions on each side. This causes the
liquid to flow from side to side across the central axis in a rhyth-
mical figure of eight.

This basic arrangement and process has been adapted into
many different forms; bigger and smaller, some asymmetrical,
some circular, others developing a theme from vessel to vessel, and
some just having one half of the vessel. They have been used for
many purposes including food processing, air conditioning, for
aesthetic settings, for treating farm wastes, for mixing the prepara-
tions of bio-dynamic agriculture, and for aerating sewage. There
are over 600 installations around the world using the Flowforms
and although some people use them for no other reason than the
aesthetics of moving water caressing a sculpted form, many have
adopted them to try and enhance the quality of the living
organisms, which the water passing through the forms can
support.

Flowforms were developed out of a world-view which
considers living organisms and their behaviour to be more than the
product of the chemical and physical elements of their bodies. The
perception that the laws of matter are inadequate to describe the
phenomena of life is complemented by the assertion of an
additional principle, which differentiates mechanisms from
organisms.

The philosophical and practical foundation for the scientific
study of such a principle was proposed by Rudolf Steiner (of
whom we wrote in chapter five) and the specific application to
water was continued by Theodor Schwenk and George Adams.
Theodor Schwenk's thoughtful observations were published in a
beautiful book called *Sensitive Chaos*, which was blessed with a
preface by Commander Jacques Cousteau. Adams' study of

SCIENCE

Flowforms

Figure 7.3.a. Akala Flowform cascade (Site System, CAT).

Figure 7.3.b. The Shamrock Flowform (treating farm waste).

Figure 7.3.c. Helena Flowform cascade.

projective geometry encouraged him to investigate whether there was any noticeable response of organisms to water which had passed over surfaces whose forms were mathematically accurate reproductions of forms found throughout nature. Working together in 1961, Schwenk and Adams enlisted the help of the sculptor John Wilkes to create the apparatus for their experimentation.

Adams' death in 1963 halted this phase of experimentation but John Wilkes, upon continued exposure to Theodor Schwenk's work with water movement, continued to pursue the ideas on an artistic basis. The outcome of John Wilkes' thought, experimentation and observation is the Flowforms.

Wilkes' Flow Design Research Group in Sussex, and allies around the world, research forms for many different installations. The work with mathematically informed surfaces has only just begun again and awaits sufficient resources to receive full investigation.

As yet it is not clear, in a statistically significant way, whether organisms and life processes benefit or are retarded by contact with water passed through Flowforms, but CAT is about to commence a comparison of how plants and creatures are affected when irrigated either from a Flowform or a simple step cascade.

Organisations with degrees of sympathy with this investigation of living phenomena often install Flowforms when an aeration device is required, or when a sculpture is considered appropriate, and sometimes when the quality of life is considered essential to a project.

The thesis under which these investigations have proceeded is not an easy bedfellow for the scientific establishment and is viewed with differing degrees of scepticism by the current authors. Indeed, were one to pursue the thesis consistently, a great deal of this book would need to be rewritten, since the premises of the Big Circle are significantly different from those of anthroposophy. (Given the opportunity, one of the present authors would love to undertake such a rewrite. Further exploration of this work was prepared but was considered to take the publication too far from its primary goal. That missing chapter is now available separately — see Resource Guide.)

Instead the authors have chosen to use the most widely adopted model of what is happening in the cycle of life and death. One can only leave it to the individual whether such a possibility of working with life *per se* is possible, and how to balance any possible benefits against the need for electric pumps, often necessary to create the constant stream of water which makes the Flowform motion manifest.

Summary

Treated sewage is a source of plentiful nutrients. This resource may be returned to selected plants and/or animals, either in the form of humus or as a liquid effluent, while simultaneously 'polishing' the sewage. There is sometimes the possibility of generating a useful harvest from it.

One option is the reintroduction of liquid effluent into life-forms after its passage through sculpted vessels — Flowforms. These add oxygen and create a pleasing rhythm in the water, which is considered by some to enhance the water's life-supporting capacity.

Conclusion

We have chosen not to labour water's ecological crisis. We feel that unending drones about melting ice caps, disappearing lakes, immortal carcinogenic pollutants and wars over control of water supplies may be numbing rather than activating. Our agenda has rather been to elucidate the details of the problems and possible solutions of sewage pollution in the hope that individuals will then be able to work better on their own corner of the crisis.

It is beyond the scope of this introduction to enter into the details of design and installation. Rather, we have offered an overview of the processes and technologies, as a *first* step to determining your treatment system requirements. We hope, that by encapsulating this exposition within a grander context — with which we can all identify — you will not only achieve a more informed position, but also embrace the matter as a challenge, with inspiration and enthusiasm.

May your Sewage Solutions answer the Call of Nature!

(Now please wash your hands.)

Glossary

Adsorption
When one substance is taken up by another adhering it to its surface.

Aerobic
Containing free oxygen (i.e. oxygen gas). Usually refers to conditions required for certain types of bacteria (aerobes) to thrive. Typically, aerobic processes require at least 1-2 mg/l dissolved oxygen.

Algae
A collection of relatively simple plants, varying in size from single cells to filamentous forms, such as 'blanket weed', to several meters in the case of some seaweeds.

Algal blooms
Extensive growths of algae indicating eutrophication. Can be a problem in sewage systems using ponds, as algae discharged in effluent will give a high suspended solids and BOD reading.

Ammonia (NH₃)
A sharp smelling gas that readily dissolves in water, forming relatively non-toxic ammonium ions (NH_4^+). Poisonous to fish and oxygen-consuming when metabolised.

Anaerobes
Organisms capable of living in the absence of free oxygen. Strict anaerobes cannot survive in the presence of oxygen.

Anaerobic
Containing no free oxygen. Anaerobic sewage smells unpleasant.

Anoxic
Without free oxygen but with nitrate (NO_3) present, which can be used by certain bacteria as a source of oxygen, so releasing nitrogen gas.

ATU
1-allyl-2-thiourea, added during the BOD test to inhibit nitrifying bacteria, so that the oxygen demand measured is due solely to the breakdown of carbonaceous (organic) matter.

Bauxite
Naturally occurring aluminium oxide, used in the production of zeolite for phosphate-free washing powders. There is some concern about the impact of open cast mining in Australia where bauxite used in the UK comes from.

Blackwater
Domestic wastewater from toilet flushings, as opposed to greywater (qv.).

Chloride (Cl⁻)
Humans excrete around 6g of chloride a day in sewage. Since treatment plants do not generally remove it, its concentration is a useful indicator of sewage pollution in a watercourse. In normal concentrations chloride is not considered harmful.

Chlorine (Cl$_2$)

Toxic yellow-green gas used to sterilise drinking water (and used in chemical warfare). The element chlorine (Cl) is found in table salt, as well as in some of the most toxic, carcinogenic and persistent chemicals made by humans, such as DDT and Dieldrin. Chlorine is responsible for huge reductions in water related illness and is implicated in the possible increase in potential carcinogens in our water.

Detergents

Products used for cleaning in solution with water, usually with the help of surfactants. Unlike soaps they are effective in hard water and tend to be less biodegradable.

Digestion

Chemical or biological process in which compounds or materials are broken down into simpler compounds.

Dip Pipe

'T'-shaped (on its side) pipe that allows liquid from below the surface to leave a tank while retaining the surface material.

Dissolved oxygen (DO)

Free oxygen dissolved in water is required for higher plants, animals and aerobic bacteria, and so a measure of the dissolved oxygen in a stream or pond can provide an indication of its health. DO is usually expressed as mg/l or as a percentage of saturation at the sample's temperature.

Effluent

Wastewater leaving a treatment system or stage of a system. (Cf. influent).

Enzymes

These proteins are produced by living cells to act as catalysts. They increase the rate of chemical reactions (such as those involved in decomposition), yet remain themselves unchanged. There are products on the market containing dried enzymes for adding to septic tanks or blocked drains, which can accelerate organic decomposition. Biological washing powders contain enzymes which are added to help digest proteins but these types of enzymes can lead to health problems in sensitive people.

Eutrophication

Enrichment of a body of water by nutrients, usually nitrates and phosphates. This can lead to excessive algal and plant growth. Phosphate is usually the limiting nutrient in fresh water and unfortunately is the hardest to remove from wastewater. Eutrophic waters lack species diversity and tend to be dominated by a few species of algae.

Facultative bacteria

Bacteria able to survive in aerobic and anaerobic conditions.

Greywater

Domestic wastewater not including toilet flushings, as opposed to blackwater (qv.).

Infiltration

In geological terms this is the vertical flow of water from the soil surface towards the water table. In sewage circles it usually refers to water entering a sewer from the ground, e.g. through broken pipes and manhole walls. Also used to describe a method of disposal to land, such as a soakaway.

Influent

Wastewater entering a treatment system or a stage of a system (cf. effluent).

Metabolism

The transformation of matter and energy in organisms. Subdivided into catabolism (qv) — the breakdown of complex organic molecules into simpler products, and anabolism (qv) — the synthesis of complex molecules from simpler ones.

Night soil
Undiluted human muck, so called because it used to be collected at night from earth closets or out-houses.

Nitrate (NO_3^-)
One of the three major plant nutrients, non toxic to aquatic life (in normal amounts) but capable of leading to eutrophication. A maximum level is set for nitrate in drinking water as it can cause 'blue baby syndrome' and it may be implicated in stomach cancer since it can form nitrite in the stomach.

Nitrite (NO_2^-)
A nitrogenous ionic molecule poisonous to fish (see ammonia and nitrate). Nitrite is highly unstable and is usually formed when nitrate is being created or broken down. Although measured in effluent samples, its concentration is of limited interest and rarely rises above 1mg/l in wastewater because of its instability.

Nutrient removal
The removal of phosphorus and nitrogen compounds in effluent to reduce the risk of eutrophication. A ratio of BOD to nitrogen and phosphorus of about 100:5:1 is required in order to optimise aerobic digestion of wastewater. Domestic sewage has a BOD:N:P ratio around 100:17:5. This means that aerobic digestion will leave an excess of N and P, which may, therefore, escape to a watercourse. Nitrogen can be removed by denitrification but phosphorus has no significant gaseous pathway and so must be removed in biomass , by adsorption or chemical precipitation.

Phosphorus (P)
Total phosphorus in domestic sewage amounts to around 2.8g/person/day of which about half is from washing powder. In eutrophication, phosphorus is usually the limiting nutrient. Algal blooms usually occur at phosphate levels greater than 0.05 mg/l in still water and 0.1 mg/l in running water. Typical sewage effluent is in the range 5-15 mg/l.

Population equivalent
Specifies the loading from places of intermittent use such as restaurants or hospitals in terms of an equivalent full-time domestic population. It is assumed that one person equivalent represents about 60g /day of BOD and about 180 l/day hydraulic loading, 10g nitrogen/day and 2.8g phosphorus.

Retention time
A measure of the average time taken for wastewater to pass through a treatment unit such as a pond, tank or reed bed. The theoretical retention time is obtained by dividing the tank volume in litres by the daily flow in litres per day. In practice, short circuiting reduces the actual retention time to around half of this for most ponds and settlement tanks.

Soap
Material used for washing; a mixture of sodium salts of stearic, palmitic or oleic acids or of the potassium salts of these acids ('soft soap '). Soaps are made by the action of sodium hydroxide (caustic soda) on fats. This is why weak caustic soda solution feels soapy; it turns your greasy finger tips into soap!

Surfactant
Short for 'surface active agent', used in conjunction with detergents as a wetting agent.

Resource Guide

This lists organisations, consultants, equipment suppliers and publications concerned with the issues described in this book.

The inclusion of any company does not constitute a recommendation for that company's products or services. Potential customers are advised to contact several companies to compare products, services and prices.

Many publications and products products listed can be ordered from the Centre for Alternative Technology Mail Order Service either by post with a cheque or on the credit card 24 hour answerphone line, 01654 703409. Postage and packing rates: goods total below £10 add 20% (min. £1); total £10-£15 add £3.00; total £15-£40 add £4.00; total over £40 add £4.50; overseas orders add 30% (minimum £1.95).

This guide is ordered as follows:

General Organisations

Consultancy

Courses

Information

Manufacturers and suppliers
Aquatic plants
Biodigesters
Cesspools
Chemical toilets
Compost toilets
Dividers and nets
General
Leachfields
Percolating filters
Rotary biological contactors
Settlement tanks
Septic tanks
Toilets
Treatment plants

Research and development

Water conservation and purification

Publications — available from C.A.T. and elsewhere

Periodicals

Note: The Water Association (WA) is a group of people from different organisations, who recognise the inseparable association between water quality and life, and whose main professional motivation is to protect or enhance water quality in the environment. Their headquarters is at Ruskin Mill. Organisations included in this guide who are members of the Association are marked *.

General Organisations

ASSOCIATION OF ENVIRONMENT CONSCIOUS BUILDING
Nant-y-Garreg, Saron, Llandysul, Caernarvonshire, SA44 5EJ
Tel/Fax. 01459 370908
Offers advice on all aspects of 'green' building. Has produced a directory of environmentally-friendlier building products and services. Members get information on environmental building in quarterly magazine *Building for a Future*.

BRITISH EFFLUENT & WATER ASSOCIATION
Now incorporated into British Water (see below), along with the British Water Industries Group (BWIG).

BRITISH WATER
1 Queen Anne's Gate, London SW1H 9BT.
Tel. 0171 957 4554   Fax. 0171 957 4565.
Water industry trade association incorporating British Effluent and Water Association, and British Water Industries Group (BWIG). Represents 400 companies

involved in all aspects of the water cycle.

CENTRE FOR ALTERNATIVE TECHNOLOGY *
Machynlleth, Powys SY20 9AZ.
Tel. 01654 702400   Fax. 01654 702782.
The Centre has over 21 years' experience with alternative sewage treatment systems, including willows and trenches, compost toilets, greywater, urine use and reed beds. Information, publications, consultancy service and courses available on reed bed design and compost toilets.

CHARTERED INSTITUTION OF WATER AND ENVIRONMENTAL MANAGEMENT
15 John Street, London WC1N 2EB.
Tel. 0171 831 3110   Fax. 0171 405 4967.
Multi-disciplinary professional and examining body for engineers, scientists and other professionally qualified personnel engaged in water and environmental management. CIWEM organises conferences and seminars, publishes a journal, newsletter and manuals on all aspects of water and waste water treatment.

DEPARTMENT OF THE ENVIRONMENT (WATER DIRECTORATE)
Romney Ho., 43 Marsham St., London SW1P 3PY.
Tel. 0171 276 8808   Fax. 0171 276 8405.
Ensures that the water companies in England and Wales provide a wholesome supply of drinking water and meet the requirements of the water quality regulations.

EFFLUENT PROCESSING CLUB (EPC)
AEA Technology, B404, Harwell Laboratory, Oxfordshire OX11 0RA.
Tel. 01235 434686   Fax. 01235 432313.
Provides a link between legislation, technology and industry. Publishes an Effluent Processing manual, giving technical advice.

FRIENDS OF THE EARTH
26-28 Underwood Street, London N1 7JQ.
Tel. 0171 490 1555   Fax. 0171 490 0881.
Campaign to maintain and enhance the quality of water. Free briefing sheets on water privatisation, nitrates and drinking water.

GREENPEACE
Canonbury Villas, Islington, London N1 2PN.

Tel. 0171 354 5100   Fax. 0171 696 0012/0014.
International, independent environmental pressure group which acts against abuse to the natural environment.

INDUSTRIAL WATER SOCIETY
Mill House, Tolson's Mill, Lichfield Street, Fazeley, Staffordshire B78 3QB.
Tel. 01827 289558   Fax. 01827 250408.
Promotes information and research about industrial and commercial water use.

INTERNATIONAL ASSOCIATION OF WATER QUALITY
1 Queen Anne's Gate, London SW1H 9BT.
Tel. 0171 222 3848   Fax. 0171 233 1197.
Membership organisation for interested parties. Produces publications and holds conferences.

NATIONAL TRUST
Estates Advisers Office, 33 Sheep St., Cirencester, Glos. GL14 1JJ.
Tel. 01285 651818   Fax. 01285 657936..
Owns, manages and conserves land and buildings of historic interest and natural beauty for the public benefit. Researching and applying appropriate solutions for minimising resource use, waste treatment and recycling.

OFFICE OF WATER SERVICES (OFWAT)
Centre City Tower, 7 Hill St., Birmingham B5 4UA.
Tel. 0121 625 1300   Fax. 0121 625 1400.
Government department responsible for ensuring the water industry provides quality/efficient service. Information service, leaflets, publications.

OXFAM
274 Banbury Road, Oxford OX2 7DZ.
Tel. 01865 311311   Fax. 01865 312600.
Carries out research and development into sanitation, water supply, latrines, etc. and produces publications on these subjects.

ROYAL COMMISSION ON ENVIRONMENTAL POLLUTION
Church Ho., Gt. Smith St., London SW1P 3BZ.
Tel. 0171 276 2080   Fax. 0171 276 2098.
Independent advisory body on principles and policies that should apply to pollution abatement and control. Produces reports on environmental pollution.

SURFERS AGAINST SEWAGE
The Old Counthouse Warehouse, Wheal Kitty, St. Agnes, Nr. Truro, Cornwall TR5 0RE.

Tel. 01872 553001 Fax. 01872 552615.
Grass roots environmental campaign
group running a high profile, media-
oriented campaign for the cessation of
sewage disposal and toxic dumping at sea.

THE SOUTHEAST CENTRE FOR THE RESTORATION OF WATERS
1 Locust Street, Falmouth, MA 02540, USA.
Tel. 0101 (508) 540 6801 Fax. 0101 (508) 540 6811.
A branch of Ocean Arks International, a
non profit making research and education
institute founded in 1981. Uses 'Living
Machines' (including portable models), for
water treatment, and uses other eco-
technologies such as fluidised beds, to
treat sewage and waste water.
Publications and education programmes.

WATER AID
Prince Consort House, 27-29 Albert
Embankment, London SE1 7UB.
Tel. 0171 793 4500 Fax. 0171 793 4545.
Charitable organisation focussing on low
cost schemes for sustainable development,
providing sanitation facilities and clean,
safe water.

WATER COMPANIES ASSOCIATION
1 Queen Anne's Gate, London SW1H 9BT.
Tel. 0171 222 0644 Fax. 0171 222 3366.
The national representative body for water
supply companies which provide water to
25% of the population of England and
Wales. Aims to represent, promote and
protect the common interests of its
members and provide a forum for
members to discuss matters of mutual
concern. *(The water supply companies were*
established in the private sector many years
ago but were brought within a new water
industry system of economic, product and
service regulation by the Water Act 1989).

WATER SERVICES ASSOCIATION
1 Queen Anne's Gate, London SW1H 9BT.
Tel. 0171 957 4567 Fax. 0171 957 4666.
Association of the ten water and sewage
undertakers in England and Wales.
Promotes their interests, provides
information and fora for discussion.

WOMEN'S ENVIRONMENTAL NETWORK
Aberdeen Studios, 22 Highbury Gr., London N5 2EA.
Tel. 0171 354 8823 Fax. 071 354 0464.
Women's environmental campaigning

group — information, education,
discussion. Perpetrators of the 'Bag It and
Bin It' campaign, to prevent the entry of
sanitary protection materials into our
watercourses.

WORLD RESOURCE FOUNDATION
Bridge House, Tonbridge, Kent TN9 1DP.
Tel. 01732 368333 Fax. 01732 368337.
Charity promoting energy recovery from
domestic waste. Publishes *Warmer Bulletin*
and factsheets on many topics including
compost and waste minimisation.

Customer Service Committees
Each region in England and Wales has its
own CSC set up by OFWAT to mediate
between the water and sewerage companies
and customers. There are ten. The telephone
numbers indicated by a * are charged at the
local rate.

OFFICE OF WATER SERVICES (OFWAT)
(See above)

OFWAT CENTRAL CSC
1st Floor; 77 Paradise Circus,
Queensway, Birmingham 81 2DZ.
Tel. 0121 212 5202 (0345 023953)*
Office hours: 8.45 am — 4.45 pm.
Responsible to customers of: Severn Trent
Water Ltd., South Staffordshire Water plc.

OFWAT EASTERN CSC
Ground Floor, Carlyle House, Carlyle Road,
Cambridge CD4 3DN.
Tel. 01223 323889 (0345 959369)*
Office hours: 9.00 am — 5.00 pm.
Responsible to customers of: Anglian
Water Services Ltd., Cambridge Water
Company, Essex and Suffolk Water plc.,
Tendring Hundred Water Services Ltd.

OFWAT NORTHUMBRIA CSC
2nd Floor, 35 Nelson Street,
Newcastle upon Tyne NEI SAN.
Tel. 0191 221 0646 (0345 089367)*
Office hours: 8.30 am — 5.00 pm Mon-
Thurs, 8.30 am — 4.30 pm Fri. Responsible
to customers of: Northumbrian Water
Ltd., North East Water plc., Hartlepool
Water plc.

OFWAT NORTH WEST CSC
Suite 902, 9th Floor, Bridgewater House,
Whitworth St., Manchester Ml 6LT.
Tel. 0161 236 6112 (0345 056316)*
Office hours: 9.00 am — 5.00 pm.

Responsible to customers of: North West Water Ltd.

OFWAT SOUTHERN CSC
3rd Floor, 15-17 Ridgmount Street, London WC1E 7AH.
Tel. 0171 636 3656 (0345 581658*)
Office hours: 9.00 am 5.30 pm Mon-Thurs, 9.00 am — 5.15 pm Fri. Responsible to customers of: Southern Water Services Ltd., Portsmouth Water plc., South East Water Ltd., Mid-Kent Water plc., Folkestone & Dover Water Services Ltd.

OFWAT CSC FOR THE SOUTH WEST
1st Floor, Broadwalk House, Southernhay West, Exeter EX1 1TS.
Tel. 01392 428028 (0345 959059*)
Office hours: 8.45 am — 4.45 pm.
Responsible to customers of: South West Water Services Ltd.

OFWAT THAMES CSC
2nd Floor 15-17 Ridgmount Street, London WC1 E 7AH.
Tel.0171 636 3656 (0345 581658*)
Office hours: 9.00 am — 5.30 pm Mon-Thurs, 9.00 am — 5.15 pm Fri. Responsible to customers of: Thames Water Utilities Ltd., Three Valleys Water plc., East Surrey Water plc., North Surrey Water Ltd., Mid-Southern Water plc., Sutton District Water plc.

OFWAT CSC FOR WALES
Room 140, Caradog House, 1-6 St Andrews Place, Cardiff CF1 3BE.
Tel. 01222 239852 (0345 078267*)
Office hours: 8.30 am — 4.30 pm.
Responsible to customers of: Dwr Cymru Cyfyngedig, Chester Waterworks Company, Wrexham and East Denbighshire Water Company.

OFWAT WESSEX CSC
Unit 2, The Hide Market, West St., St. Phillips, Bristol BS2 0BH.
Tel. 0117 955 7001 (0345 078268*)
Office hours: 8.45 am — 4.45 pm.
Responsible to customers of: Wessex Water Services Ltd., Bournemouth and West Hampshire Water plc., Bristol Water plc., Cholderton & District Water Company Ltd.

OFWAT YORKSHIRE CSC
Symons House, Belgrave Street,
Leeds LS2 8DF.
Tel. 0113 234 0874 (0345 089368*)
Office hours: 8.30 am — 5.00 pm.
Responsible to customers of: Yorkshire Water Services Ltd., York Waterworks plc.

WATER SERVICES ASSOCIATION
(See above)

Regulatory Authorities

If you are installing an independent treatment system you may need to inform the following bodies:

YOUR LOCAL AUTHORITY
See your local phone book.
Any of the following departments may need to be informed and consulted: Building Regulation, Environmental Health, Planning and Technical services.

England & Wales
THE ENVIRONMENT AGENCY
Rivers House, Waterside Drive, Aztec West, Almondsbury, Avon BS12 4UD.
Tel. 01454 624400 Fax. 01454624409.
Organisation resulting from the merger of the National Rivers Authority, the Waste Regulation Authorities, Her Majesty's Inspectorate of Pollution and several smaller units from the Department of the Environment. Aims to provide a comprehensive approach to the protection and management of the environment by combining the regulation of land, air and water. *(Emergency hotline 0800 807060 covers all of England and Wales.)*

Northern Ireland
ENVIRONMENT HERITAGE SERVICE
Calvert House, 23 Castle Place, Belfast, Northern Ireland BT1 1FY.
Tel. 01232 254754 Fax. 01232 254700.
Aims to maintain and develop water and sewage services to required quality and environmental standards to Northern Ireland. Offers publications such as factsheets, brochures and research reports.

Scotland
SCOTTISH ENVIRONMENTAL PROTECTION AGENCY
1 South Street, Perth, Scotland PH2 8NJ.
Tel. 01783 627989 Fax. 01783 630997.
Government body that aims to provide a comprehensive approach to the protection and management of the Scottish environment.

Consultancy

A.R.M. Ltd.
Rydal Ho., Colton Rd., Rugeley, Staffs. WS15 3HF.
Tel. 01889 583811 Fax. 01889 584998.
Designs aerobic treatment systems for agricultural, industrial and domestic waste materials using reed beds and various composting processes including commercial use of the 'Armix' composting machine which speeds up the composting process. Carries out research with Birmingham University.

ABRAHAMS JULIAN
Thistledown Cottage, Hope House Lane, Stanford Bishop, Worcester WR6 5TZ.
Tel. 01886 884721 Fax. None.
Design of 'Wetland Ecosystem Treatment' system which treats waste water using constructed wetlands on domestic, agricultural and industrial scales. Also teaches permaculture.

ACER ENVIRONMENTAL CONSULTANTS Ltd.
Acer House, Brooklands, 680 Budshead Road, Plymouth PL6 5XR.
Tel. 01752 769675 Fax. 01752 769677.
Environmental consultancy, laboratory and scientific services company, specialising in water and environmental management, land development, analytical testing, policy statements, environmental audits and risk assessment. Part of the Acer Group of companies, owned wholly by Welsh Water plc.

ACQUISITION & ENVIRONMENTAL
Bywater House, 16 East Street, Didcot, Oxfordshire OX11 8EJ.
Tel. 01235 815221 Fax. 01235 812551.
Specialises in acquisition audits for the legal and finance sectors, although legal compliance audits and baseline studies for BS7550 also play a major part. Also covers waste issues, environmental management and strategic studies.

ASPINWALL & COMPANY Ltd.
Walford Manor, Baschurch, Shrewsbury SY4 2HH.
Tel. 01939 262200 Fax. 01939 262222.
Environmental management consultant. Carries out research in areas of waste management.

ATKINS (W.S.) CONSULTANTS
Longcross Court, 47 Newport Rd., Cardiff CF2 1AD.
Tel. 01222 485159 Fax. 01222 485138.
Consultancy service in water treatment, supply, sewer treatment, environmental, hydraulics, project appraisal, water industry management.

BINNIE & PARTNERS
Grosvenor House, 69 London Road, Redhill, Surrey RH1 1LQ.
Tel. 01737 774155 Fax. 01737 772767.
Provides professional engineering service in the collection, treatment and disposal of waste water.

BIO SYSTEMS INTERNATIONAL Ltd.
Empire House, Beauchamp Avenue, Kidderminster, Worcestershire DY11 7AQ.
Tel. 01562 825800 Fax. 01562 825801.
Advice, process design, project control in effluent/waste-water management.

BURNHAM ENVIRONMENTAL SERVICES
27 Brightstowe Road, Burnham-on-Sea, Somerset TA8 2HW.
Tel. 01278 786104 Fax. 01278 793380.
Supplies/installs small treatment plants including its own low power Biodigester. Consultancy service. Specialises in systems for small populations.

CAMPHILL WATER*
C.V.T. Ltd., Oaklands Park, Newnham-on-Severn, Gloucestershire GL14 1EF.
Tel. 01594 516063 Fax. 01594 516821.
Offers consultancy, planning, design, research, setting up and commissioning of reed beds, ponds and compost toilets. Runs 5 day sewage treatment course for lay-people which covers theory, design and installation of aquatic plant and composting systems.

CENTER FOR THE PROTECTION AND RESTORATION OF WATERS
Now called Watershed Systems. See below.

CENTRE FOR ALTERNATIVE TECHNOLOGY
(See General Organisations).

CLEANWATER
Foxfield, Welcombe, Bideford, N. Devon EX39 6HS.
Tel. 01288 331561 Fax. 01288 331561.

Installs small package sewage treatment — all sorts of management — septic tanks, reed beds, etc. Consultancy service. Services cover all of Wales and Southern England.

CORY ENVIRONMENTAL Ltd.
25 Wellington Street, London WC2E 7DA.
Tel. 0171 379 9090   Fax. 0171 379 8053.
Analysis, treatment and disposal of domestic/industrial waste.

CRESS WATER
37 Harrow Rd, St. John's, Worc., WR2 6BX.
Tel/Fax. 01905 422707.
Consultancy, designs, installs reed beds, wetlands, ponds for treating domestic-industrial wastewater effluents. Potable water conservation/filtration.

DE TWAALF AMBACHTEN
De Bleken 2, 5282 HB Boxtel, Netherlands.
Tel. 0031 4116 72621   Fax 0031 4116 72854.
Produces composting loos, advice on reed beds, provides good DIY plans.

DUNTECH ENVIRONMENTAL SERVICES
Chinnor Rd., Towersey, Thame, Oxon. OX9 3QZ.
Tel. 01844 215411   Fax. 01844 261353.
Design and management of reed beds.

EASTWOOD SERVICES
Kitty Mill, Wash Lane, Wenhaston, Halesworth, Suffolk IP19 9DX.
Tel. 01502 478249   Fax. 01502 478165.
Agent for biological and urine separating toilets, especially 'Biolet' and 'Ekologen'. Consultant for domestic water conservation and recycling systems.

EBB & FLOW*
Ruskin Mill, Nailsworth, Glos. GL6 0LA.
Tel. 01453 836060   Fax. 01453 835029.
Designs and builds dirty water treatment systems using flowform ponds and wetlands. Gives lectures.

ENVIRONMENTAL BIOTECHNOLOGY Ltd.
PO Box 129, Bridgwater, Somerset TA5 1YR.
Tel. 01278 671527   Fax. 01278 671567.
Consultancy service on trade/domestic effluent and environmental engineering. Design and project management. Reed bed systems, industrial effluent, composting, anaerobic digestion and waste minimisation.

ENVIRONMENTAL SCIENCES UNIT
ESU Services Ltd., 4 Cumberland House, Greenside La., Bradford, W. Yorkshire BD8 9TF.
Tel. 01274 480033   Fax. 01274 544491.
Consultant for reed beds, presently monitoring ICI's Billingham and British Steel beds. Involved with reed bed projects in UK and Australia. Joint organisation with Oceans Environmental Engineering Ltd.

GRANT, NICK
Withy Cottage, Little Hill, Orcop, Hereford HR2 8SE.
Designer, adviser and installer of custom made dosing siphons. Consultancy on reed beds, other forms of sewage disposal and water conservation. Publication available.

IRIS WATER & DESIGN*
Langburn Bank, Castleton, Whitby YO21 2EU.
Tel. 01287 660 002   Fax. 01287 660 004.
Designs and installs waste water systems — including ponds and reed beds. Largest UK agents for flowforms (attractive stone sculptures shaped to allow oxygenation and revitalisation of treated water). Designs and manufactures own model of flowforms.

LIVE WATER TRUST*
c/o Alan Hall, Hawkwood College, Painswick Old Road, Stroud, Gloucestershire GL6 7QW.
Tel. 01452 814054   Fax. 01452 525667.
Researches and promotes an understanding of the life-giving quality of water. Send SAE for details.

LIVING TECHNOLOGIES Ltd.
The Park, Findhorn, Moray IV36 0TZ.
Tel. 01309 691258   Fax. 01309 691387.
Constructs and markets large scale (200 people plus) 'Living Machines', which are biological wastewater treatment systems.

LIVING WATER*
5 Holyrood Rd., Edinburgh, Scotland EH8 8AE.
Tel. 0131 558 3313   Fax. 0131 558 1550.
Ecological waste water systems — domestic and industrial. Consultancy service.

MONTGOMERY WATSON
201 Amersham Road, High Wycombe, Buckinghamshire HP13 5AJ.
Tel. 01494 526240   Fax. 01494 522074.

International consulting engineers for water, wastewater and the environment. Also involved with industrial and hazardous waste management.

OCEANS ENVIRONMENTAL ENGINEERING Ltd.
4 Cumberland House,
Greenside Lane, Bradford BD8 9TF.
Tel. 01274 480033. Fax. 01274 544491.
Works as part of the Environmental Sciences Unit. Consultant for both types of reed bed systems.

REEDBED TECHNOLOGY Ltd.
324 Manchester Road, West Timperley
Altringham, Cheshire WA4 5NB.
Tel. 0161 969 8881. Fax. 0161 969 4441.
Reed bed consultancy, including design and installation. Solids collection tanks. Emphasis on ecosystems, often involving aquaculture and anaerobic digestion — biogas yielded.

ROBERTSON LABORATORIES
Llanrhos, Llandudno, Gwynedd LL30 1SA.
Tel. 01492 581811 Fax. 01492 592030.
Accredited laboratory providing analytical services to the environmental sector for water, wastewater, air pollution, soil and contaminated land testing.

SAC ENVIRONMENTAL
Bush Estate, Penicuik, Edinburgh EH26 0PH.
Tel. 0131 535 3075 Fax. 0131 535 3070.
Advice, design and project management on waste water management in general, and reed beds and constructed wetlands in particular. R&D and consultancy in effluent and waste water management.

SHELBARN SERVICES
46 Market Street, Oakengates,
Telford, Shropshire TF2 6DU.
Tel. 01952 617855 Fax. 01952 618274.
Supplies and installs reed bed systems, especially for Severn Trent Water plc. Other lines of work include clean water and sewage treatment.

THE SOUTHEAST CENTRE FOR THE RESTORATION OF WATERS
(See General Organisations).

TINSLEY BERRY Ltd.
Leo House, 14 — 16 St. Nicholas Church
Street, Warwick CV34 4JD.
Tel. 01926 496656 Fax. 01926 407244.

Installer of sand/gravel reed beds. Consultancy and design work as well on commercial and domestic scale. Also constructs large scale wetlands.

WATER, ENGINEERING & DEVELOPMENT CENTRE
Loughborough University of Technology,
Loughborough, Leicestershire LE11 3TU.
Tel. 01509 222622 Fax. 01509 211079.
Education, training, research and consultancy for the planning, provision and management of water supplies and sanitation for less developed countries.

WATER RESEARCH CENTRE, plc
Henley Road, Medmenham,
Marlow, Buckinghamshire SL7 2HD.
Tel. 01491 571531 Fax. 01491 579094.
A leading European research, technology and consultancy company, in the fields of water, wastewater and environmental management. Customers include government agencies, international organisations and companies with business interests covering a range of industrial sectors. Occasionally runs courses. WRc Alert is the commercial environmental consultancy arm of WRc plc.

WATERSHED SYSTEMS Ltd.
Technology Transfer Centre, Kings Buildings,
Mayfield Road, Edinburgh EH9 3JL.
Tel. 0131 668 1550 Fax. 0131 662 4678.
(Taken over The Centre for the Protection and Restoration of Water UK). Research/development/installation of waste water treatment systems. Living machines (solar aquatics), a pond/reed bed/Flowform system.

WETLANDS ADVISORY SERVICE Ltd.
Wildfowl and Wetlands Trust,
Slimbridge, Gloucestershire GL2 7BT.
Tel. 01453 890030 Fax. 01453 890827.
Consultant on wetland management and assessment. Also studies reed bed systems.

Courses

CAMPHILL WATER
(See Consultancy).

CENTRE FOR ALTERNATIVE TECHNOLOGY
(See General Organisations).

CHARTERED INSTITUTION OF WATER AND ENVIRONMENTAL MANAGEMENT
(See General Organisations).

INSTITUTE OF IRRIGATION STUDIES
University of Southampton,
Southampton, Hampshire SO20 1BJ.
Tel. 01703 593728   Fax. 01703 677519.
Runs an MSc course on 'Engineering for Development' which includes a core module on sanitation and sewage.

SILSOE COLLEGE — CRANFIELD UNIVERSITY
Silsoe, Bedford, Bedfordshire MK45 4DT.
Tel. 01525 860428   Fax. 01525 863001.
Environmental Water Management course (MSc). Aims to facilitate evaluations of water related ecological systems for cost effective engineering solutions.

UNIVERSITY OF ABERTAY, DUNDEE
Waste Water Dept., Bell Street,
Dundee, Scotland DD1 1HD.
Tel. 01382 308000   Fax. 01382 308877.
Wastewater and Environmental Management MSc. Reflects current and future problems in wastewater and environmental management. Monitoring and control of environmental pollutants and water.

WATER RESEARCH CENTRE, plc
(See Consultancy).

Information

BRITISH SOCIETY OF DOWSERS
Sycamore Barn, Hastingleigh,
Ashford, Kent TN25 5HW.
Tel/Fax. 01233 750253.
Has a quarterly journal, lectures and meetings on the use of dowsing for geophysical, medical, agricultural and other purposes. Booklist available.

CENTRE FOR ALTERNATIVE TECHNOLOGY
(See General Organisations).

CHARTERED INSTITUTION OF WATER AND ENVIRONMENTAL MANAGEMENT
(See General Organisations).

DE TWAALF AMBACHTEN
(See Consultancy).

EFFLUENT PROCESSING CLUB (EPC)

(See General Organisations).

FRIENDS OF THE EARTH
(See General Organisations).

GREENPEACE
(See General Organisations).

INDUSTRIAL WATER SOCIETY
(See General Organisations).

MURRAY-DARLING FRESH-WATER RESEARCH CENTRE
P.O. Box 921, Albury 2640, Australia.
Tel. 060 431002   Fax. 060 431626.
Research primarily on wastewater treatment using artifical wetlands for single houses or small communities. Collaborative ventures with industry.

OFFICE OF WATER SERVICES
(See General Organisations).

RUSKIN MILL*
Ruskin Mill, Nailsworth, Glos. GL6 0LA.
Tel. 01453 832571   Fax. 01453 832571.
Manufactures flowforms designed by the Flowform Design Association UK and also provides environmental information.

THE SOUTHEAST CENTRE FOR THE RESTORATION OF WATERS
(See General Organisations).

WASTE MANAGEMENT INFORMATION BUREAU
AEA Technology,
National Environmental Technology Centre,
F6, Culham, Abingdon, Oxon. OX14 3DB.
Tel. 01235 463162   Fax. 01235 463004.
Provides comprehensive information /advice service on all aspects of waste management, from commercial hazardous waste disposal to domestic disposal.

WATER COMPANIES ASSOCIATION
(See General Organisations).

WATER, ENGINEERING & DEVELOPMENT CENTRE
(See Consultancy).

WATER SERVICES ASSOCIATION
(See General Organisations).

WOMEN'S ENVIRONMENTAL NETWORK
(See General Organisations).

WORLD OF WATER
Number Six, Fourth Ave., Birmingham B29 7EU.
Tel. 0121 471 2363   Fax. 0121 472 7372.

Aims to improve the attitude to water life and the total water environment.

WORLD RESOURCE FOUNDATION
(See General Organisations).

Manufacturers and suppliers

Aquatic plants

ANGLO AQUARIUM PLANT Co. Ltd.
Strayfield Road, Enfield, Middlesex EN2 9JE.
Tel. 0181 363 8548 Fax. 0181 363 8547.
Major producer and supplier of a whole range of aquatic plants.

LONDON AQUATIC Co. Ltd.
Greenwood Nursery, Theobolds Park Road, Enfield, Middlesex EN2 9DH.
Tel. 0181 366 4143 Fax. 0181 367 6256.
One of the most reliable suppliers and growers of the full range of aquatic plants. Also installs reed beds for road run-off.

MERTON HALL POND Ltd.
Merton, Thetford, Norfolk IP25 6QH.
Tel. 01953 881763 Fax. 01953 884020.
Major grower and supplier of aquatic plants of all species.

STAPLEY WATER GARDENS Ltd.
Stapeley, Nantwich, Cheshire CW5 7LH.
Tel. 01270 623868 Fax. 01270 624919.
Huge garden centre specialising in aquatic plants.

YARNINGDALE NURSERIES
16 Chapel Street, Warwick CV34 4HL.
Tel. 01926 496656 Fax. 01926 407244.
Supplies reeds for reed bed systems suitable for local area. Supplied reeds for beds at C.A.T. Designs and installs septic tank systems and industrial sewage treatment plants (work connected with Tinsley Berry Ltd).

Biodigestors

For further information on suppliers of aerobic digesters in your area check the Yellow Pages under Sewage Treatment.

MALTIN POLLUTION CONTROL SYSTEMS (1967) Ltd.
Gould's Ho., Horsington, Somerset BA8 0EW
Tel. 01963 370100 Fax. 01963 371300.
Supplies energy-efficient 'Cardioid Digester Systems' for the anaerobic transformation of all forms of organic waste into useful by-products (methane,

fertilisers, etc.) while treating many types of farm and industrial effluents.

Cesspools

For further information on suppliers in your area check the Yellow Pages under cesspools.

Chemical toilets

For further information on suppliers in your area check the Yellow Pages under Chemical Toilets.

Compost toilets

BARTON ACCESSORIES
Morleigh Road, Harbertonford, Totnes, Devon TQ9 7TS.
Tel/Fax. 01803 732878.
Supplies (worldwide) the WEB (waterless electronic biological) toilet.

CAMPHILL WATER*
(See Consultancy).

CENTRE FOR ALTERNATIVE TECHNOLOGY *
(See General Organisations).

CLIVUS MULTRUM Inc.
Harvard Square, 104 Mt. Auburn Street, Cambridge, MA 02138, USA.
Tel. + 1 617 491 0051 Fax. + 1 617 491 0053.
Manufactures the Clivus Multrum compost toilet. See Kingsley Clivus, below.

DE TWAALF AMBACHTEN
(See Consultancy).

EASTWOOD SERVICES
(See Consultancy).

KINGSLEY CLIVUS COMPOSTING UK.
Kingsley House, Woodside Road, Boyatt Wood Trading Estate, Eastleigh, Hampshire SO50 4ET.
Tel. 01703 615680 Fax. 01703 624613.
UK supplier and distributor for the Clivus Multrum range of composting toilets and greywater systems.

OXFAM
(See General Organisations).

SANCOR INDUSTRIES Ltd.
140-30 Milner Avenue, Scarborough, Ontario, Canada M1S 3R3.
Tel. (416) 299 4818 Fax. (416) 299 3124.
Manufacture and supply a range of 'Envirolet' composting toilets, including waterless self-contained systems, low water and waterless remote systems.

WENDAGE Ltd.
Rangeways Farm, Conford,
Liphook, Hampshire GU30 7QP.
Tel. 01428 751296   Fax. 01428 751541.
Supplies various models of self-contained
electric compost toilet — 'Biolet', which
can include urine separation. Also
bacterial augmentation systems.

Dividers and nets

BORIS NET CO.Ltd.
Copse Road, Fleetwood, Lancashire FY7 6RP.
Tel. 01253 874891   Fax. 01253 778203.
Supplier of custom made polythene cargo
nets for solids lifting, (e.g. from solids
collection tanks.)

CENTRIFORCE
86 Blackpole Trading Est.,Worcs. WR3 8SQ.
Tel. 01905 455410   Fax. 01905 754708.
Supplier of recycled polythene rigid
sheets, useful as dividing walls, etc. for
reed bed construction.

ERMIN PLANT
Bristol Road, Gloucester GL2 5DF.
Tel. 01452 526616   Fax. 01452 304099.
Supplier of debris nets for solid collection,
filtering and lifting.

HUESKER SYNTHETIC
11 Welham Road, Great Bowden,
Market Harborough, Leicestershire LE16 7HS.
Tel/Fax. 01858 463646.
Supplier of liners comprising bentonite
sandwiched between two geosynthetic
membranes — good for lining reed beds.

LEDATEC (GEOTEXTILES)
Longshaw Industrial Park,
Highfield Road, Blackburn BB2 3AS.
Tel. 01254 56413   Fax. 01254 682723.
Produces and supplies needle punched,
non-woven fabrics.

MONARFLEX GEOMEMBRANES Ltd.
Lyon Way, St. Albans, Hertfordshire AL4 0LB.
Tel. 01727 830116   Fax. 01727 860045.
Manufactures and supplies polythene
liners appropriate for use with reed beds.

PAXTON
Newfield Close, Green Lane, Walsall WS2 7TB.
Tel. 01922 726060   Fax. 01922 643422.
Supplies medium density polyethylene
tanks which can be used for reed beds.

THE TANK EXCHANGE
Lewden House, Barnsley Road, Dodworth,
Barnsley, South Yorkshire S75 3JU.
Tel. 01226 203852   Fax. 01226 206157.
Supplier of polyethylene, recycled
containers for settlement tanks and
compost bins. Supplies rain water
recycling equipment.

General

ECO CLEAR
Appledram, Lane South, Chichester, West
Sussex PO20 7PE.
Tel. 01243 533838   Fax. 01243 533178.
Liquid waste management and drainage
contractor.

PLANTS FOR A FUTURE
The Field, Higher Penpol, St. Veep.
Lostwithiel, Cornwall PL22 0NG.
Tel. 01208 873554   Fax. none.
Charity and permaculture specialists
providing a selection of 1800 useful trees,
shrubs and perennial vegetables by mail
order.

SEEFLOW OVERFLOAT
Yorkshire House, Canal Bridge, Sykes Lane,
Silsden, West Yorkshire BD20 0EB.
Tel. 01535 653444   Fax. 01535 654867.
Manufactures and supplies internal
overflow systems.

Leachfields
Look up under Builders and sewage in your
local Yellow Pages.

Percolating filters
For further information on suppliers in your
area check the Yellow Pages.

Rotary biological contactors
Check the Yellow Pages for other suppliers.

TUKE & BELL Ltd.
Beacon Street, Lichfield, Staffs. WS13 7BB.
Tel. 01543 414161   Fax. 01543 250462.
Designs, manufactures and installs sewage
treatment plants and sewage purification
equipment, worldwide, available in the
form of fixed biological contactors,
rotating biological contactors and a system
of biological treatment by rotating filters.
Other types of equipment include
mechanical and bubble type aeration
systems and ancillary equipment.

Settlement tanks
For further information on suppliers in your
area check the Yellow Pages.

PEGLER VALVES
PO Box 182, St. Catherines Avenue, Doncaster, South Yorkshire DN4 8DN.
Tel. 01302 739595   Fax. 01302 730517.
Supplies 4" gate valves for sludge.

Septic tanks
Septic tank leachfield systems treat sewage well and have many applications. For further information on suppliers in your area check the Yellow Pages under septic tanks.

Toilets
See also Compost toilets.

EASTWOOD SERVICES
(See Consultancy).

GLOBEMALL Ltd.
1 Woodbridge Road, Ipswich IP4 2EA.
Tel. 01473 259232   Fax. 01473 286285.
Manufactures the 'Ernst Waterless H_2NO! Urinal'. A unique protective bactericidal coating prevents even the smallest drops of urine from remaining on the surface. The result is a totally hygienic odour-free urinal without using a drop of water.

IFO SANITAR AB
Box 140, S-29500, Bromolla, Sweden.
Tel. +46 456 480 00   Fax. +46 456 480 48.
Manufactures water-conserving, low-flush (3.5 litre) toilet cisterns. Supplied in this country by Camphill Water (see Reed Beds and Consultancy).

VILLEROY & BOCH
267 Merton Road, London SW18 5JS.
Tel. 0181 871 4028   Fax. 0181 870 3720.
Dual flush low water consumption toilets.

Treatment plants
For further information on suppliers in your area check the Yellow Pages.

ALBION CONCRETE PRODUCTS
Pipe Ho. Wharf, Morfa Rd., Swansea SA1 1TD.
Tel. 01792 655968   Fax. 01792 644461.
Supplier of concrete rings (with or without lid and base) for reed beds, solid collection.

BCM CONTRACTS Ltd.
Unit 22, Civic Industrial Park, Whitchurch, Shropshire SY13 1TT.
Tel. 01948 665321   Fax. 01948 666381.
Supplier of glass reinforced cement tanks and troughs, e.g. for reed beds, solids collection, etc.

BURNHAM ENVIRONMENTAL SERVICES
(See Consultancy).

CLEANWATER
(See Consultancy).

EBB & FLOW
(See Consultancy).

ECL
Stirling House, Danebury Court, Old Sarum Park, Old Sarum, Wiltshire SP4 6EB.
Tel. 01722 413339   Fax. 01722 413306.
Designs and manufactures a wide range of specialist systems and products for sewage and waste water treatment.

IRIS WATER & DESIGN
(See Consultancy).

LAKE AID SYSTEMS
Bridge House, St. Germans, Kings Lynn, Norfolk PE34 3ES.
Tel. 01553 617030   Fax. 01553 617718.
Supplies aerator systems and wind pumps.

LIVING TECHNOLOGIES Ltd.
(See Consultancy).

SHELBARN SERVICES
(See Consultancy).

TINSLEY BERRY Ltd.
(See Consultancy).

TUKE & BELL Ltd.
(See Rotary biological contactors).

WENDAGE POLLUTION
(See Compost toilets).

YARNINGDALE NURSERIES
(See Manufacturers and suppliers).

Research and development
ASPINWALL & COMPANY Ltd.
(See Consultancy).

BHR GROUP Ltd.
Cranfield, Bedford MK43 0AJ.
Tel. 01234 750422   Fax. 01234 750074.
R&D into processes of dealing with liquids, slurries and suspended solids.

BIOTECHNA-GRAESSER A.P. Ltd.
20 New Bond Street, London W1Y 9HF.
Tel. 0171 495 4812   Fax. 0171 495 4810.
Uses chlorella algae to absorb nutrients such as nitrogen and phosphate from effluent and turn them into protein.

BIOTECHNICAL CLEANING
P.O. Box 181, Abingdon, Oxon. OX14 4YS.
Tel. 01235 848909   Fax. 01235 848909.
Uses bacteria and fungi to cleanse soils contaminated by industrial processes and waste. Most work in the UK done on landfill sites.

CAMPHILL WATER
(See Consultancy).

CENTRE FOR ALTERNATIVE TECHNOLOGY
(See General Organisations).

**ECOLOGY ACTION
(OF THE MID PENINSULA)**
5798 Ridgewood Road,
Willits, CA 95490 — 9730, USA.
Tel. 001 707 459 0150.   Fax. 001 707 459 5409.
23 years of research into sustainable food production including complete recycling of human urine and faeces into soil.
Publishes *Future Fertility — Transforming Human Waste into Human Health, (available from Camphill Water).*

FLOWFORM DESIGN ASSOCIATION UK*
Emerson College, Hertfield Road, Forest Row, East Sussex RH18 5JX.
Tel. 01342 824080 Fax. 01342 823078.
Designs and researches water movements and invented flowforms.

IMBACH BIOLOGICAL SERVICES
Westgate, Aldridge, West Midlands WS9 8EX.
Tel. 01922 743585 Fax. 01922 58813.
Uses bacteria to control environmental pollution.

INDUSTRIAL WATER SOCIETY
(See General Organisations).

KASSEL UNIVERSITY
Dept. of Eco-Chemistry, Monchebergstr.
No. 19, Post Fach 010380, Kassel, Germany.
Tel. 0049 5618040.   Fax. 0049 8042330.
Where horizontal flow reed bed systems were originally researched by Dr. Kickuth and vertical flow ones by Dr. Seidel.

LIVE WATER TRUST
(See Consultancy).

MURRAY-DARLING FRESH-WATER RESEARCH CENTRE
(See Information).

OCEANS ENVIRONMENTAL ENGINEERING Ltd.
(See Consultancy).

SAC ENVIRONMENTAL
(See Consultancy).

SCHOOL OF CHEMICAL ENGINEERING
University of Birmingham, Edgebaston B15 2TT.
Tel. 0121 414 5292/0 Fax. 0121 414 5324.
Composting and reed bed research for 25 years. Works with A.R.M. Ltd. and Yarningdale Nurseries.

SCHOOL OF CIVIL ENGINEERING
Portsmouth University, Burnaby Building,
Burnaby Rd., Portsmouth, Hampshire PO1 3QL.
Tel. 01705 842424 Fax. 01705 842521.
Researching, in conjunction with Camphill Water and Montgomery Watson, gravel bed hydroponics (using effluent to grow food, incorporating industrial effluent).

THE SOUTHEAST CENTRE FOR THE RESTORATION OF WATERS
(See General Organisations).

WATER, ENGINEERING & DEVELOPMENT CENTRE
(See Consultancy).

WATER RESEARCH CENTRE, plc
(See Consultancy).

WATERSHED SYSTEMS Ltd.
(See Consultancy).

WENDAGE POLLUTION
(See Compost toilets).

WMC RESOURCE RECOVERY Ltd.
2 Eaton Cres., Clifton, Bristol, Avon BS8 2EJ.
Tel. 0117 973 7993 Fax. 0117 973 3167.
Biological digestion treatment of household domestic waste including sewage. The products of this process are used to produce a horticultural growing medium, fibrous material for flatboard and moulded products industries, and combined with coal dust to produce a blended fuel. The energy required to operate this process is provided by biogas released from the waste materials during the conditioning process.

WOODS END RESEARCH LABORATORY
37 Crandos Rd., Stroud, Gloucestershire GL5 3QT.
Tel. 01453 763299 Fax. 01453 751473.
Active research into the way in which

different waste materials produce different types of compost, and the effect of compost on soils and crops. Provides a comprehensive resource planning and management service on this subject.

Water conservation

See also Toilets

CAMPHILL WATER
(See Consultancy).

CRESS WATER
(See Consultancy).

EASTWOOD SERVICES
(See Consultancy).

FREEWATER UK Ltd.
Peak House, Shepley Lane,
Marple, Cheshire SK6 7JW.
Tel. 0161 449 7220/1 Fax. 0161 449 7242.
Franchise company offering systems for grey and rain water recycling.

GRANT, NICK
(See Consultancy).

HYDREC
Woodside House, 7 Woodside Green,
London, SE25 5EY.
Tel. 0181 655 1696 Fax. 0181 654 8302.
Manufactures and installs domestic grey water systems.

MEP CONTROLS
Hill House, 36 Rayne Road,
Braintree, Essex CM7 7QP.
Tel. 01376 323122 Fax. 01376 323109.
Supplies 'Aqualite' water management system, to save water and lighting costs in public or workplace toilets.

PREMIAIRE plc
The Rise, Stow Road, Purleigh,
Chelmsford, Essex CM3 6RR.
Tel. 01621 829600 Fax. 01621 829700.
Supplies the 'Pressure Butt', which allows capture of rainwater and re-use of grey-water for garden and/or flushing toilets. Approved by the Water Research Council.

THE GREEN SHOP
Bisley, Stroud, Gloucestershire GL6 7BX.
Tel/Fax. 01452 770629.
Has a catalogue of environmentally and ethically aware products. Supplies 'Wisy-Filter Collectors': filters and collects rain water to provide water for toilet, washing machine, household cleaning, garden, etc.

Water purification

AQUA CURE plc
Aqua Cure House, Hall Street,
Southport, Merseyside PR9 0SE.
Tel. 01704 501616 Fax. 01704 544916.
Manufacturer of water filter systems and purifiers for domestic and industrial use.

ARBOUR TECH Ltd.
Kingsland, Leominster, Herefordshire HR6 9SF.
Tel. 01568 708840 Fax. 01568 708974.
Water purification by ultraviolet and/or filtering.

CRESS WATER
(See Consultancy).

EVERPURE WATER FILTERS: CITMART
Lympne Industrial Park, Hythe, Kent CT21 4LR.
Tel. 01303 262211 Fax. 01303 260057.
Supplies water filters.

LIFF INDUSTRIES Ltd.
Bayhall, Miln Road, Huddersfield,
West Yorkshire HD1 5EJ.
Tel. 01484 512537 Fax. 01484 513597.
Water treatment products, including water softeners, water filters, ultraviolet disinfection units and scale inhibitors.

SHAKESBY & SONS Ltd.
97 Angela Rd, Horsford,
Norwich, Norfolk NR10 3HF.
Tel. 01603 262263 Fax. 01603 262161.
Supplier of filter systems for private water supplies.

THE FUNDAMENTAL ENERGY COMPANY
Fieldway Limited, Croft Road,
Crowborough, East Sussex TN6 1DL.
Tel. 01892 655782 Fax. 01892 655792.
Manufactures an electronic water purifier (the 'Self-Compensating Electronic Water Purifier') which converts dilute sewage to potable water, redces hardness, replaces chlorine in purifying swimming pools, removes *Legionella* bacteria from wet air conditioning systems. It works by passing a low voltage current between electrodes, ionising the water.

VERTAC INDUSTRIES
Unit 16, Halcyon Court, St Margarets Way,
Huntingdon, Cambs. PE18 6EB.
Tel. 01480 411185 Fax. 01480 413747.
Designer, manufacturer and supplier of water filters and softeners.

Publications available from C.A.T. Mail Order

C.A.T. Publications

Safe to Drink? The Quality of Your Drinking Water   £7.95
Julie Stauffer, New Futures 8 (1996) 160pp.
Accessible book covering what is in your tapwater, treatment systems, the efficacy of filters and bottled waters, conservation, greywater use, and getting an independent supply from spring, well, rain or stream. Also examines if the UK has enough water, the behaviour of the water suppliers and how to complain. Well illustrated. Resource Guide. Glossary.

Fertile Waste   £3.95
Peter Harper, New Futures 3 (1994) 28pp.
Managing your domestic sewage. Compost toilets, septic tanks, other ways of turning your sewage problems into solutions. Includes a UK guide to suppliers and further information.

The Reed Beds at C.A.T   £1.95
Jeremy Light & Chris Weedon, (1995) 12pp.
A collection of four articles from C.A.T's *Clean Slate* magazine about the two reed bed sewage treatment systems serving the C.A.T. site and the Eco Cabins.

Constructed Reed Beds Tipsheet   £0.30
Answers to frequently asked questions about our pioneering reed bed sewage treatment systems.

Water Conservation in the Home Tipsheet   £0.30
How to save water and use it more wisely.

Making Use of Waste Water Tipsheet £0.30
Tips on how to re-use your household 'greywater'.

Recycling Resource Guide   £0.70
Details of organisations, consultants, equipment suppliers and manufacturers, courses and publications concerned with aspects of the recycling of many kinds of materials.

Other Books

Affordable Water Supply and Sanitation   £15.95
Ed. Pickford, Barker, Code, Dijkstra, Elson, Ince, Shaw; IT Publications in conjunction with Water Engineering Development Centre (1995) 171pp.

How to Shit in the Woods   £5.99
Kathleen Mayer, Ten Speed Press (1994) 107pp.
Written with an effervescent sense of humour, this is a book for anyone who wants to enjoy the outdoors, responsibly.

Natural Garden Book   £14.99
Harper & Light, (1994) 288pp.
Systematically lays out the range of choices in your garden – from wildlife to recreation and healing plants to vegetable growing, plus lots of fascinating biological and social background material.

Sanitation Without Water   £5.95
U.Winblad, Macmillan (1993) 158pp.
Very popular guide to composting toilets and urine use, etc.

Septic tanks: An overview   £5.00
N. Grant & M. Moodie, Nick Grant (1995) 16pp.
Covers soakaway pits and leachfields, dosing, rain water and water use.

The Toilet Papers   £8.95
Sim Van der Ryn, Ecological Design Press (1995) 127pp.
An informative, inspiring and irreverent look at how people have dealt with human wastes over the centuries, and at what safe designs are available today that reduce water consumption and avert the necessity for expensive treatment systems.

The Worth of Water   £9.95
John Pickford, IT Publications (1991) 136pp.
Technical briefs on health, water and sanitation, including septic tank and latrine design. Excellent for developing countries.

Water Treatment and Sanitation   £5.95
Mann & Wilson, IT Publications (1982) 96pp.
Excellent handbook for anyone involved in small-scale water supply and waste systems. Design information on wells, pipes, pumps, filters, toilets and sewage treatment.

The following are <u>not</u> available from C.A.T Mail Order

A Diagnostic & Ecological Approach to the Purification of Sewage, Toxic Substances and Water Bodies
Ehrlich, M-C. Cantin & A. Turcotte (1991) 14pp.
Technical but important discussion of the use of micro-organisms in 'solar aquatic' and Bacta-Pur purification systems. (Available from Aquaresearch Ltd. Send contribution plus postage).

Agriculture:
A Course of Eight Lectures   £9.10
Rudolph Steiner, Agriculture Association (1977) 175pp.
Given to agriculturalists familiar with Steiner's basic concepts, the discussions between the lectures cover human muck. Lecture eight touches upon the rationale for Steiner's caution.

A New Community Approach to Waste Water Treatment with Higher Plants £1.70
U. Burka & P. C. Lawrence, Camphill (1990) 12pp.
A talk given at the Cambridge International Conference on Constructed Wetlands. A technical paper on the design and performance of the two Oakland Park systems examining their relevance to wider municipal and industrial waste treatment. (Available from Camphill Water).

A Technical paper on research in Australia by the Murray-Darling Centre.
(Available from the Water Research Centre or the Murray-Darling Centre. Send contribution plus postage).

Biological Degradation of Wastes £120.00
Martin, (1992) 429pp.
Attempts to provide comprehensive coverage of biodegredation of solid wastes, gaseous effluents and liquid wastes.

Biology of Waste Water Treatment £80.00
N.F. Gray, Oxford University Press (1992) 828pp.
An academic book covering the biological processes of this subject.

Biological Wastewater Treatment Systems: Theory and Operation   £19.95
N.J. Horan, Wiley (1989) 320pp.
A very cost-effective text book on conventional sewage treatment that provides much background information for the would-be designer and installer.

Bioremediation   £59.90
Baker, (1992) 320pp.
Overview of basic science and engineering involved in using micro-organisms to mitigate, control and reverse the effects of chemical pollutants in the environment.

British Code of Practice for Design and Installation of Small Scale Sewage Treatment Works and cesspools. BS6297.
          £61.50
British Standards Institution (1983) 40pp.

Cleaning Up   £7.95
Elkington & Shopley, World Resources Institute (1989) 92pp.
US waste management technology and third world development.

Clean Clothes and the Environment £5.50
Jenny Allen, Women's Environmental Network (1993) 90pp.

Constructed Wetlands in Water Pollution Control   £93.50
P.F. Cooper & B.C. Findlater, Pergamon Press (1990) 640pp.
Proceedings on the 1990 International Conference on the Use of Wetlands in Water Pollution Control. Very large collection with a few relevant papers. (Available from the Water Research Centre, send for their large publications list too).

Constructed Wetlands for Waste Water Treatment   £76.90
Hammer, CRC Press (1989) 800pp.
Conference reports.

Design and Operation of Small Wastewater Treatment Plants   £80.00
IAWQ, Pergamon (1993) 385pp.
Selected conference proceedings from Trondheim, Norway 28-30th June 1993. Vol. 28, No. 10 of the Water, Science & Technology Journal.

Dirty Man of Europe: The Great British Pollution Scandal   £9.95
Rose, Simon & Schuster (1991) 366pp.
A damning look at Britain's environmental pollution record.

Earthworms in Waste and Environmental Management   £100.90
Edwards & Neuhauser, (1988) 392pp.
This book presents papers on the areas where use of earthworms could be greatly beneficial.

East Anglian Privvies.   **£6.95**
Jean Turner, Countryside Books (1995) 128pp.
A nostalgic trip down the garden path.

**Ecological Engineering for Waste Water
Treatment**   **£32.00**
C. Etnier & B. Guterstam, Bokskogen (1991) 366pp.
Proceedings of an international conference:
learned and progressive information.
(Available from Bokskogen, Box 7048, S-
402, 31 Gothenburg, Sweden. Add £4.25 for
postage).

**Effluent and Waste Water Treatment
Technology**   **£25.00**
Magazine supplement guide to the
sanitation industry, includes list of
companies for mainstream technology.
(Available from Environment Business
Magazine 0181 877 9130. Price dependent
on number ordered).

**Effluent Treatment
and Waste Disposal**   **£34.40**
Handley, Hemisphere (1990) 411pp.

**European Design and Operational
Guidelines for Reed Bed Treatment
Systems U117**   **£10.00**
Water Research Centre (1990).
Specific guide to horizontal systems.
(Available from the Water Research
Centre.)

**European Pollution Control and Waste
Management Industry
Directory: 1992**   **£395.00**
POLMARK Compiled by ECOTEC, (1992) 650pp.
Country-by-country directory of
companies; full products and services
index.

Flowforms   **£3.50**
Mark Moodie, Camphill Water (1990) 17pp.
The long chapter/essay omitted from this
publication. (Available from Camphill
Water.)

Flowforms and the Language of Water
Mark Reigner & John Wilkes, (1989) 7pp.
Article written for Towards Journal, Vol.3
No.2. (Available from 3442 Grant Park
Drive, Carmicheal, CA 95608, USA).

**Function of Macrophytes in Constructed
Wetlands**   **£80.00**
H. Brix, Pergamon (1994) 8pp.
Taken from Water Science and Technology
Journal, Vol. 29, No.4. The price is for the
whole journal and not just the relevant
article.

**Future Fertility: Transforming Human
Waste into Human Health**   **£22.00**
John Beeby, Camphill Water (1995) 164pp.
The exhaustive research work on recycling
human waste.

Greywater Use in the Landscape   **£4.00**
R. Kourik, Edible (1988) 28pp.
A useful booklet, oriented to California
conditions. (Available from PO Box 1841,
Santa Rosa, CA 95402, USA. Add £1.00 for
postage).

Kompost — Toiletten   **£16.00**
Ladener Okobuch, Freiburg (1992) 163pp.
The most complete account yet on
composting toilets, but only for those who
read German.

Mega Slums: The Coming Sanitary Crisis
                               FREE (donation)
Maggie Black, Water Aid (1996) 30pp.
One of a series of reports by Water Aid on
global water and sanitation problems.
(Available from Water Aid, 1 Queen
Anne's Gate, London, SW1H 9BT. Send
large SAE).

**Plants for Reclamation
of Wastelands**   **£125.00**
Sastry et al., (1990) 684pp.
Covers the use of 1003 plant species in
India.

**Reed beds and Constructed Wetlands for
Wastewater Treatment**   **£80.00**
*PM Cooper, GD Job, MB Green, RB Shutes,
WRc plc, (1996) 192pp.*
Horizontal and vertical reed beds:
description, theory and pracrtice, planting,
design, performance; with case studies.

Septic tanks and cesspools   **£14.95**
P. Jobling, Peter Jobling Publishing (1994) 136pp.
A do-it-yourself guide. (Available from
Glandewi, Meidrim, Carmarthen, Dyfed,
SA33 5PD).

**Treatment, Disposal and Management of
Human Wastes**   **£65.00**
*Matsumoto & Matsuo,
Pergamon Press (1987) 428pp.*

**The Real Goods Solar
Living Source Book**   **£18.50**
Ed. John Schaeffer, Chelsea Green (1994) 672pp.

**The Nature and Properties of Soils
(9th edition)** £14.95
*Brady & Bachman, Collier Macmillan (1984)
560pp.*

**Use of Macrophytes in Water Pollution
Control (The)** £36.95
Athie & Cerri, Pergamon Press (1988) 186pp.
An academic book on the use of macro-
phytes to control water pollution.

Waste in Troubled Waters
*Leonie Crennan, University of Tasmania —
Environmental Studies Working Paper #22.*
The case for dry sewage treatment and a
good section on cultural paradigms and
taboos. (Only available from the Board of
Environmental Studies, University of
Tasmania, Tasmania, Australia.)

**Wastewater Engineering, Treatment,
Disposal, Re-use** £36.95
Metcalf & Eddy, McGraw (1990) 1024pp.
A cost effective text book on conventional
sewage treatment that provides much
background information for the would-be
designer and installer.

**Wastewater Treatment for Pollution
Control** £10.95
Arceivala, McGraw (1987) 187pp.

Wastewater Treatment Publications£395.00
Published by the Murray-Darling Centre.
An annotated bibliography, Australian
based. (Available from the Murray-Darling
Centre.)

**Water Supplies and the Treatment and
Disposal of Effluents** £4.00
Little & Harold, Textile Institute (1975)

**Water Supply Bylaws Guide —
2nd Edition** £7.95
*Ed. S.F. White & G.D. Mays,
Water Research Centre (1989) 250pp.*
(Available from Water Byelaws Advisory
Service at the Water Research Centre (see
Consultancy). Complete guide to
accpetable practices for all aspects of
plumbing, supply and treatment.

Periodicals

Industrial Waste Management £44.00
*Ed. Angela Himus, Faversham House,
111 St. James Road, Croydon, Surrey CR9
2TH.*
Treatment and supply, industrial waste,
news freebie for the industry, subscription
or otherwise.

Institution of water officers
*Heriot House, 12 Summerhill Terrace,
Newcastle-upon-tyne NE4 6EB.*
Technical feature articles, Institution news
and reports and articles of a general
interest for senior management and
engineers within the water and waste
industries.

Water & Environment International £60.00
*Ed. Jim Manson, International Trade
Publications Ltd., Queensway House, 2
Queensway, Redhill, Surrey, RH1 1QS.*
Bimonthly, subscription. Supply,
sanitation and the environment, world-
wide developments.

Water and Waste Treatment £42.00
*Ed. Victoria Mitchell, Faversham House,
111 St. James Road, Croydon, Surrey CR9
2TH.*
Supply and sanitation industry freesheet;
news and developments. Monthly, free to
industry, subscription or otherwise.

Water Bulletin £50.00
*Ed. Paul Garrett, Water Services Association,
1 Queen Anne's Gate, London SW1H 9BT.*
Trade news weekly for supply and
sanitation, published by the water service
companies' trade association. Weekly,
subscription.

Water Products
*Faversham House, 232a Addington Road,
Selsdon, South Croydon CR2 8LE.
Tel. 0181 651 7100 Fax. 0181 651 7117.*
Aimed at water and waste water treatment
industry. Focuses on new products,
services and technological developments.

Water Quality International £98.00
*Pergamon Press, Headington Hill Hall,
Oxford OX3 0BW.*
Academic. Also produces *Water Services*
and *Water Supply* publications.

Water Science & Technology Journal —

1996 Edition   **£1,690**
Available from Pergamon Press.

Water Services International   **£92.00**
*Ed. Jim Manson, International Trade
Publications Ltd., Queensway House,
2 Queensway, Redhill, Surrey, RH1 1QS.*
Business magazine for management,
engineers, and consultants. Technical news
developments. Also publishes the annual
Water Services Yearbook. Monthly, free to
industry, subscription or otherwise.

Wet News
*Turret House, 171 High Street,
Rickmansworth WD3 1SN.*
Newspaper for the water and effluent
treatment industries.

**World Water & Environmental
Engineering**
*Faversham House, 232a Addington Road,
Selsdon, South Croydon CR2 8LE.*
Publication covering all aspects of the
water industry, from developing nations to
industrialised areas.

WWT Water & Waste Treatment
*Faversham House, 232a Addington Road,
Selsdon, South Croydon CR2 8LE.*
Magazine covers all aspects of the water
industry from potable water to the
treatment of effluent.

Index

N E W FUTURES

A series from CAT Publications

The following books are in this series. It is intended to form a comprehensive guide to environmental living, and we recommend obtaining the whole set. Titles are continually being published and updated — the anticipated dates are in brackets.

General

Eternal Energy in the Real World Horne, B and Peasley, E (August 1997) NF5, 128pp, £7.95

Careers and Courses in Sustainable Technologies Shepherd, A (1995), NF7, 96pp, £5.95

General Technology

Off the Grid: Managing Independent Renewable Electricity Systems Allen, P and Todd, R, (1995) NF6, 60pp, £5.50

Power Plants: A Guide to Biofuels Horne, B (1996) NF16, 64pp, £5.50

Wind Power

Where the Wind Blows: An Introduction to Wind Power Horne, B, (1994), NF9, 28pp, £3.50

It's a Breeze — A Guide to Choosing Windpower Piggott, H (1995), NF13, 36pp, £4.50

Windpower Workshop, Piggott, H (January 1997), NF14, 160pp, £6.95

Water Power

Going with the Flow: Small Scale Water Power Langley, B and Ramsey, R (February 1997), NF15, 120pp, £7.95

Solar Power

Tapping the Sun: A Solar Water Heating Guide Horne, B (1994), NF1, 16pp, £2.50

Solar Water Heating: A DIY Guide Trimby, P (1994), NF10, 32pp, £3.95

Wired Up to the Sun: A Guide to the Photovoltaic Revolution, Allen, P (1994), NF4, 32pp, £3.95

Energy Conservation

Save Energy Save Money: A Guide to Energy Conservation in the Home, Jackson, F (1995), NF2, 40pp, £4.50

Environmental Building

Out of the Woods: Ecological Designs for Timber Frame Self Build Borer, P and Harris, C (1994), NF11, 124pp, £12.50

Home and Dry: Ecological Building Design and Materials Borer, P and Harris, C, (March 1997) NF18 192pp, £9.95

Transport

Getting There: Navigating the Transport Maze Kelly, R (March 1997), NF21, 128pp, £7.95

The Food Cycle

Safe to Drink? The Quality of Your Water Stauffer, J (1996), NF8, 160pp, £7.95

Sewage Solutions: Answering the Call of Nature Grant, N, Moodie, M and Weedon, C (1996), NF12, 160pp, £8.95

Fertile Waste: Managing Your Domestic Sewage, Harper, P (1994) NF3, 32pp, £3.95

The Ground Rules: Natural Gardening for All, Harper, P (June 1997) NF24, 92pp, £7.95

THE CENTRE FOR ALTERNATIVE TECHNOLOGY

... has been empowering people with practical, positive ways to improve their environment for 21 years.

You can —

- visit our 10 acre centre where interactive displays demonstrate wind, solar, water and bio-power, sewage treatment, organic gardening, energy conservation, self build and environmental building;

- attend any number of our many residential courses;

- experience 'green living' first hand, as a group, in our purpose built Eco-cabins;

- come as part of a group or school visit, which, where arranged, can include an introductory lecture and guided tour;

- 'buy green by mail' with our extensive mail order service including CAT's own publications;

- Join 5000 others in the rapidly expanding Alternative Technology Association, and keep up to date;

- contact our Information Department for any queries you may have;

- commission our team of highly experienced consultants — no job too big or small.

Help make a better future. Call us, visit us, write to us, use us!

**Machynlleth, Powys
SY20 9AZ, UK
Tel. 01654 702400**

**Fax. 01654 702782
Email: cat@gn.apc.org
http://www.foe.co.uk/CAT**